TODAVÍA MÉXICO

ISBN 978-0-578-62057-2

Library of Congress Cataloging-in-Publication Data
Gille, Judith
Todavía méxico: life beyond the border /
Judith Gille.—1st edition.
p. cm.
1. Mexico—Description and travel. 2. Mexico—social life and customs.
3. Title

Several of the essays in this book have appeared in anthologies or online literary journals or have been performed. "In Gracia's Kitchen" and "The Trouble with Walls" appeared in the anthologies *Connected* and *Uncommon Chord*, published by Wising Up Press. "Oaxacan Mercy" was published in *The Oasis Journal*. A version of "Disaster Gawking" was published under the title "The Ballot Party" in an anthology titled *States of the Union*. And "Submitting to El Chapo" was performed at the San Miguel Writers' Conference's Literary Death Match in 2019.

Note to the Reader:
    Some names of people in this book have been changed for various reasons. And while it is based on true events, "Portrait of a Migrant Worker" is a work of fiction.

— JG

Printed in the U.S.A.

Davis Bay Press
1011 Davis Bay Road
Lopez, WA 98260

Cover and book design by Patricia García Arreola.
Photographs, including the cover photo, by Judith Gille

TODAVÍA MÉXICO

Life Beyond the Border

JUDITH GILLE

Davis
Bay
Press

For my mother,
who never gave up on me.

CONTENTS

PART I ❀ ABRAZOS

In Gracia's Kitchen	3
¡Ojala!	9
Portrait of a Migrant Worker	11
At La Mesa Grande	23
Dreaming of Paris	25
How to Write About Your Mexican Housekeeper	29
The Lump	33
Machita	37

PART II ❀ VIAJES

Ixchel & the Fertility Goddesses: From A to Z	43
The Trip to Taninul	53
A Visit to Casa Trotsky	65
Oaxacan Mercy	73
Chiapan Journal	87

PART III ❀ DESVIACIONES

Strange Days	95
Submitting to El Chapo	111
Disaster Gawking	117
The Trouble with Walls—Part I	127
A #MeToo Near Miss	137

PART IV ❀ BENDICIONES

Chapulines	155
The Night Billy Collins Stole Alejandra's Poem	163
Death Comes to the Callejón	167
El Día de los Muertos	175
The Trouble with Walls—Part II	181

At the end of life, our questions are very simple:
Did I live fully? Did I love well?
— Jack Kornfield

PART I ❀ ABRAZOS

The author with her goddaughters

The problem with the world is that we draw
our family circle too small.
— Mother Theresa

In Gracia's Kitchen

I'VE BEEN HUNCHED OVER MY COMPUTER all morning editing an essay and need to stretch my legs and quench a thirst that is ever-present on Mexico's arid Central Plateau. I stroll across the alley, where I live in San Miguel de Allende, to my friend Gracia's store in search of sparkling water or a Sidral apple soda. But the doors to her tiny *tienda* are closed. Her youngest son, a kid named Sebastian who we all call Cholo (which translates as *Homey*), squats on the steps above me bouncing a soccer ball between his legs. He points up to the kitchen: his mom is up there.

GRACIA'S KITCHEN LIES at the back of her house and is reachable only from an outside set of concrete steps. I make the steep climb, not only because I need a drink, but because it's our daily habit to check in with each other. I check in with her because her house is lively and full of people I care about. She checks in with me, I suspect, because she thinks I'm lonely and a bit pathetic, and this is somewhat true. My husband doesn't like Mexico as much as I do and rarely comes down to San Miguel, and my adult children are too busy with their own lives to visit. Hence, I live alone in Mexico for much of the year.

"It must be sad," Gracia once said, gazing sympathetically at me with those big dark eyes of hers, "to have no family nearby."

TODAY, A BURST OF LAUGHTER fills the air as I enter her kitchen. Gracia's daughter-in-law Verónica and her stout, pretty mother,

Concha, are there. Lupe, Gracia's daughter, who is eight months pregnant, is also there. The group is gathered around a sturdy wooden dining table with a *telenovela* playing on a TV that sits beneath a pious-looking portrait of Christ at the far end of the dining table. The TV is often tuned to a soccer match or a baseball game, and sometimes to a telenovela, the soap operas my Mexican neighbors adore. Today a rerun of *Los Ricos También Lloran* is playing with the sound turned down. *Los Ricos* is one of the longest running and most popular telenovelas in Mexico, but the Mexican obsession with it baffles me. I've often wondered how working-class people can empathize with the spoiled, ultra-rich, blonde Mexicans depicted in the series. When I asked Gracia why poor and middle-class Mexicans would care about spoiled, rich people, she looked at me and shook her head: "It doesn't matter if you're rich or you're poor, everyone has problems."

GRACIA'S KITCHEN IS DIVIDED in two by a massive breakfast bar covered in cream-colored Talavera tiles. On the far side of the bar are a refrigerator, a sink, and a propane stove. Today she is busy preparing a simple cuisine: *caldo de pollo con verduras* with hot tortillas. She speaks in her usual rapid-fire Spanish as she stirs the soup and rinses plates.

"¡Hola, *Judith! ¿Tienes hambre?* Can I get you some soup?" she asks.

"*Sí, por favor,*" I say, accepting the bowl she hands me. A clear broth with pieces of chicken and lightly cooked fresh vegetables, it's delicious.

"Have you heard the news, Judith?" Lupe says, barely able to keep a straight face. "Don Octavio has a girlfriend."

"You're kidding!" I say, shocked by this news. I try to imagine poor, ancient, arthritic Don Octavio, who nearly died of a stomach infection just a few months ago, carrying on an affair under the omniscient gaze of his wife Doña Rosa. Doña Rosa epitomizes the expression "a force to be reckoned with." The sheer power of her steely glance causes people and animals on our alley to shrivel.

"Does Doña Rosa know?"

"*¡Sí!*" Gracia crows. "Elena says Doña Rosa wants to kick him out!"

During a neighborhood fiesta at Señora Juana's house this past weekend, Don Octavio kept staring at me. I assumed it was because I was the only *gringa* there and he saw me as an intruder. Now I begin to wonder what might have been going through his mind.

"I hear he's getting a little senile," I say. "Maybe he's confused and thinks he's Don Juan, instead of Don Octavio." The table erupts in laughter all over again.

Our conversation eventually turns more serious. Concha, who lives in Oaxaca, has returned to San Miguel because Verónica's father, Concha's second husband, is gravely ill with liver cancer.

"He was a hard-drinking man and *un mujeriego* like Don Octavio," Verónica says of her father.

"*¿Mujeriego?*" I've not heard this Spanish word.

"*Sí. Un mujeriego.* A man who has a lot of women."

"Aha!" I say, realizing that *mujeriego* means womanizer.

FOR THE NEXT HOUR we sit around the table discussing a subject women all over the world talk about around kitchen tables: men and their miscreant ways. Concha tells us how her first husband nearly beat her to death…on their wedding night.

"*Pos,* after beating me up, the *cabrón* disappeared for a week on a drunken spree!"

I tell them how my friend Martha's first husband disappeared on a three-day cocaine binge on their wedding night. The five of us agree, this kind of behavior is not limited to men in Mexico or the U.S. It happens all over the world.

"My dad used to hit us," Lupe says so quietly I can barely hear her. "But he doesn't do it anymore."

I've long suspected that Lupe's father might have hit Gracia and the kids, but this is the first time either of them have admitted it. Years ago, my daughter came back from their house and told me she'd seen him raise his hand to strike Gracia, but he stopped suddenly. I suspect the shocked expression on my daughter's nine-year-old face might have humbled him. Whatever the case, he stopped dead in his tracks and walked away. I also know that since those days, Lupe's father has learned skills for coping with his anger and has developed more patience and insight with age. His children might have once been afraid of him, but his grandchildren and my dogs adore him. And he's not the only one who's changed. Gracia, too, has changed.

"If anybody tried to lay a hand on me or my kids today, I'd grab a bat and start swinging," she says, imitating a home-run hitter right there in front of her refrigerator.

IN A SPIRIT OF FEMALE SOLIDARITY, I tell everybody about a *New York Times* article I read that morning that said that, due to increasing educational and employment opportunities, Mexican women are now having an average of only two children. The reporter claims the changing self-image of women is transforming cultural norms south of the border, just as it did for my generation of women in the U.S. in the late 1960s and 1970s. The way self-esteem and positive self-images continue to transform women's lives all around the world.

My mention of the NYT article launches a new discussion about how many kids is the right number to have.

"Juan wants a boy. He says if this one's a girl, we should try again," Lupe says, patting her watermelon of a belly. "But I'm done. No more babies for me!"

"One's enough," says Verónica. "I'm going back to school as soon as I can earn enough money to put Danny in daycare."

The conversation reminds me of a question that's baffled me for the many years I've lived in San Miguel, but never had the audacity to ask my Mexican friends: why don't more women on our callejón have eight or ten or twelve children like many of the mothers in the solidly Catholic neighborhood where I grew up in Chicago?

The majority of my Mexican women friends are devout Catholics. They attend mass every chance they get and always on Sunday. They gather to recite prayers on Friday nights and sometimes invite me to join them. They've walked the hundred-mile pilgrimage to the sanctuary at San Juan de los Lagos and visited the Basílica de Guadalupe in Mexico City. They cross themselves at every opportunity, obey the mandates of their local clergy, and consider the Pope a spiritual rock star.

Still, most of the young Mexican women I know have only two children, and my middle-aged friends, an average of four. Could it be that even the most pious Mexican women are ignoring the Vatican's orders and taking control of their reproductive lives?

AFTER THE OTHERS HAVE LEFT and Gracia and I are alone in her kitchen, I decide to finally pop the question.

"Gracia, there's a mystery I wish you would clear up for me."

"*¿Un misterio?*" A look of anticipation fills her face. Gracia is always intrigued by the idea of problem-solving and loves setting me straight on all things Mexican.

"Why don't more women in Mexico have eight or ten or twelve children like they did a generation ago?"

"That's simple," she says with a shrug, "they take the pill." I can tell she's a little disappointed my question was so easy.

"But how do they get around the Catholic church?"

"Well, when I was first considering taking the pill, I went to the priest and confessed."

"What did he say?"

"He told me I should make an appointment to talk with the church counselors."

"Did you?"

The look on her face reminds me of a kid who admits he stole a piece of candy, and while he feels some small sense of remorse, he still hasn't forgotten just how good it tasted.

"So you never went?"

She shakes her head, then quickly adds: "At least I confessed! Young girls today, they don't even bother to confess!"

THE CONVERSATION TURNS to whether I think birth control pills are bad for you. Not morally, but medically. She wants to know if taking them will give her cancer.

"I'm no expert," I say, "but I don't think so." I tell her that women in the U.S. have been taking the pill for more than fifty years and most of them have had no problems. This fact impresses her and, I hope, eases her fears though I suspect she won't have to worry too much longer. Having passed through the post-menopausal portal myself nearly ten years ago, I recognize its telltale signs in my friend. At the fiesta on Sunday, I noticed her face suddenly flushed bright red and small beads of sweat formed on her brow. It wasn't due to the weather or the spicy *chiles* she's so fond of; we were eating chicken in a mild *mole* sauce and the air was cool. She's also more curt and less patient these days, another sign that she's in the throes of "the big change." But I decide not to ask how she feels about menopause. I figure my friend Gracia and I have traveled far enough on the subject of women's reproductive lives for one day.

¡Ojala!

A Visit to the Electrical Supply Store

OFTEN, WHEN I RETURN to Casa Chepitos after a six-month hiatus, I find half the light bulbs in my Mexican home burned out. Maybe it's the power surges that are common in San Miguel de Allende, or maybe the renters leave them on and Balbina doesn't notice because she cleans by day. Whatever the reason, I've become a regular customer at the electrical supply store a few doors down from the ancient gas pump at the corner of Mesones and Juárez streets.

The shelves of the small shop are piled high with light bulbs, porcelain fixtures, dimmer switches, switch plates, sockets, plugs, wire, and a tangle of lamps in various states of disrepair. There are even a few small appliances—blenders, mixers, desk fans— for sale.

But my favorite thing about the shop is *la dueña*: the stooped, gray-haired, wisecracking woman who owns it. Though in her late seventies or maybe early eighties, la dueña is still as spry and sassy as a seventeen-year-old. Her deeply lined face has a rouge-inspired glow and there's a mischievous twinkle in her pale eyes. Occasionally I've seen someone who might be her son or daughter in the store, but mostly she works alone. If she has a husband, I haven't seen him in the fifteen years I've been doing business with her.

La dueña likes to joke with her customers. She even jokes with me sometimes. When she sells a bulb, no matter whether it's to an American or a Mexican, she insists on testing it in front of the customer. Trust is not high in Mexico, even among

Mexicans, and unlike in the United States where returns are ubiquitous, returning merchandise after you've walked out of a store with it is next to impossible in Mexico. I owned retail hardware stores in the U.S. for thirty-seven years and we had days where, for the first hour, we had no sales, only returns. By ten a.m. we'd be in the hole.

ONE DAY I DISCOVERED that the lights in the upstairs hallway of my Mexican house had burned out yet again. Determined to replace all the incandescent bulbs at Casa Chepitos with compact fluorescent bulbs, I trotted down the hill to visit la dueña and find out if she stocked CFLs.

La dueña keeps the small television in her store tuned to *telenovelas* or Oprah-style Mexican daytime shows. When I arrived to ask about CFL bulbs, I found her fixated on the television sitting on her counter. A middle-aged couple was fiercely debating some topic with the show's hostess when suddenly the woman—who I assumed was the man's wife—jumped up and started chasing her husband around, furiously swinging her four-inch stiletto at his head.

"*¿Qué está pasando?*" I asked la dueña, wondering why the woman was so angry.

"Her husband cheated on her," she said in Spanish.

"Looks like she's going to kill him if she catches up with him."

"*¡Ojalá!,*" la dueña said with a wink. God willing.

Portrait of a Migrant Worker

IN MANY WAYS Juan Jesús García was just like any other Mexican boy. He and his seven siblings grew up on a five-hectare farm bordering a tiny village on Mexico's Central Plateau. Puerto de Nieto, the pueblo where his family lived, had four unpaved streets, three *tiendas*, and a parochial church painted white and sky blue: the colors of *la Virgen María*.

Life was simple, though never easy, for the small wiry kid with skin the color of walnut shells and a face shaped like the moon. His father died of liver disease when he was twelve and his mother soon remarried. Luckily for Jesús and his siblings, their stepfather was a docile man, and not prone to drunken rages like their father. Together, Jesús's stepfather and mother eked out a living growing corn and alfalfa, and raising goats and chickens on the semi-arid scrap of land the family referred to as *el rancho*.

At home there was usually something to eat—tortillas, beans, maybe a little chicken or pork on fiesta days—but there was little money for "extras," like new shoes, clothing, or medicine. Because of public education laws enacted in the 1930s, Jesús and his siblings attended primary school. But without money for books or paper or pencils, they had difficulty keeping up, and by middle school his older sisters and brothers had all dropped out.

This was where Jesús was different—different from his siblings and different from other Mexican boys his age. Unlike his friends, he liked school. He *wanted* to continue. Jesús was naturally good at math—he enjoyed solving the algebraic puzzles. He also liked to draw. As a boy, he scoured the roadsides and arid arroyos for glass soda bottles he could return to the town's three tiendas to collect the centavos he needed to buy paper and pencils. His favorite things to sketch were the grand house, private chapel, and pomegranate trees belonging to Puerto de Nieto's *hacendado*. Jesús dreamed of going to a school where he could learn how to design houses like the one belonging to the town's wealthy landowner.

If I'd been born into a rich family like this, I could be anything I wanted to be, Jesús, now age fourteen, thought one day as he sketched the arched porticos surrounding the hacendado's house. But Jesús's family wasn't rich or even middle-class. They were as poor as the soil in Puerto de Nieto's four dusty streets, and when he shared his aspirations with his mother, she said: "We are not dreamers, Jesús. Dreams are for rich people. Be satisfied with what you have."

STILL, JESÚS HAD HIS HEART SET on attending high school in Querétaro or San Miguel. He thought about it day and night and studied hard so he'd be able to keep up with the city kids. Then, in his fifteenth year, the year he planned to enter *la preparatoria*, his mother and stepfather told him they could no longer support him or his education and he was forced to join the other teenage boys cruising construction sites and farms around Puerto de Nieto in search of decent jobs that didn't exist. Some of his friends left for Monterrey or Saltillo to work in *maquiladoras*, the giant factories owned by multinational corporations. Others migrated *al Norte,* to the U.S.

In 2006, the year he turned nineteen, Jesús grew tired of scrabbling for bits of occasional work that paid less than a hundred pesos a day and called his oldest sister who lived in Virginia with her husband. Jesús's brother-in-law had learned to build houses the American way and made ten times what Jesús did.

"If I come to Virginia can I learn to build American houses, too?" Jesús wondered aloud to his sister from three thousand kilometers away.

"*Tal vez, Chuy,*" she replied. Maybe.

Jesús began soliciting everyone he knew—his sisters and brothers, aunts, uncles, cousins, and friends—for the money he needed to pay a *coyote* to guide him across the Río Bravo into Texas.

"I'll pay you back when I get a job in Virginia," he promised. It took him eight months, but eventually he collected the fifteen thousand pesos he needed. His cousin, Jorge, had a friend, who had a friend, who knew a guy—the man who could lead him across the big river under the mantle of night.

❀ ❀ ❀

JESÚS KISSED HIS GIRLFRIEND LUPITA goodbye, gave his sad-eyed mother a hug, and boarded a bus bound for San Fernando de las Presas in the state of Tamaulipas. It was the first time the nineteen-year-old had been away from home. To calm his jumpy nerves, he fondled the silver crucifix Lupita had given him and quietly recited the Rosary over and over as the bus rumbled northward toward the U.S. border.

DARKNESS ARRIVED at the same hour Jesús did in San Fernando. On a designated corner, across from the bus station, he met up with the *coyote* and driver who demanded half of their payment up front, then they hustled him into the back of a rusted-out, windowless Econoline van where six men and two sloe-eyed Purepecha women from Michoacán huddled on long wooden benches. They were dressed in clothes to match the night and carried small backpacks and bottles of water. They stared at Jesús as he climbed aboard but were as silent as an Olmec monolith.

Around midnight the driver dumped them out in the desert south of Matamoros where there were no lights, no villages, no signs of life. Nothing but *echeveria,* sagebrush, and cactus grew there. Under a sky lit by distant stars, the Mexicans trudged single file along a narrow path. The only sounds were the monotonous crunch of gravel beneath their tennis shoes, the chirp of crickets, and the occasional *yip* of a coyote. Unlike the rare peaceful moments he'd enjoyed on starlit nights in Puerto de Nieto, to Jesús, the darkness and silence felt like a fifty-kilo weight. A few miles north, in a place where the Río Bravo flowed wide but not too deep, he would have to muster the courage to wade across the river and into the United States. But first, he and the others had to follow *el coyote*—a man they trusted less than a wild dog—across a vast and desolate landscape.

IT WAS A LONG, COLD, LONELY NIGHT. The loneliest night Jesús could remember. He ate his last tortilla and discovered he was almost out of water. To comfort himself he thought about Lupita's pretty smile, her soft skin, her supple breasts. He also thought about his mother and how sad she looked as he'd hugged her goodbye. He thought about his friends, and his brothers and sisters, and how all that was familiar seemed so far away.

In a litany of whispered prayers, Jesús pleaded for divine help to get him and the others across the border safely. He prayed to San Judas Tadeo for protection from the robbers and federal police who preyed on migrant workers. He prayed to the Virgin of Guadalupe that rattlesnakes and copperheads would not cross their paths. He prayed that the river would be shallow where they crossed because he and the others couldn't swim. Most of all, he prayed the coyote did not run away and that God would help them evade *la migra*—the U.S. Border Patrol.

JESÚS'S PRAYERS WERE ANSWERED. By noon the following day, he was boarding a Greyhound bus in Brownsville, Texas, bound for Prince William County, Virginia.

Shopping malls the size of small cities. Grocery stores the size of factories. Row upon row of houses *tan grande* with gardens greener and more lush than the Parque Juárez in San Miguel. Jesús was seduced by the abundance outside the window of the bus taking him to the place called Manassas, in Virginia, the state where his sister lived.

People as rich as the hacendado must live in all these fancy houses, he thought as he stared out the bus's window. Even in poorer neighborhoods, the small houses were tidy and had neatly mown emerald lawns, white fences, and smooth concrete sidewalks. No garbage strewn in the streets, no used plastic bags flapping in the breeze or broken bottles dotting the fields like in Mexico. In America, it seemed, everyone drove new cars and trucks, and had tiny telephones they carried around and talked into incessantly. Some even had computers, barely larger than sketchbooks, which they held on their laps and tapped away on, the way hens at home pecked at corn in the yard. *Yo quiero vivir como éste*, Jesús thought. I want to live like this.

IN MANASSAS HE SOON FOUND WORK on a construction site, where one hundred and forty townhouses were being built. "My name is Chuy," he told the site supervisor, in the thickly accented English he'd been practicing with his sister. "You have work for me?" The boss, a gringo named Dwayne, gave him the job of gofer to the roofers. A job no one else wanted.

Though they too were Mexican, the roofers treated Jesús with indifference and worked him at a breakneck pace ten hours a day. Lugging bales of composite shingles, fifty-pound rolls of tar paper, and boxes of roofing nails up wobbly extension ladders. The roofers were paid by the square yard: the faster they worked, the more money they earned. Jesús made six dollars an hour, no matter how fast he worked. Still, it was more money than he had ever made before and three times what he earned in Mexico. He was suddenly feeling rich, thinking of all the U.S. dollars he would make.

On his first payday, he went shopping with his sister. He bought himself a pair of Nikes, blue jeans, and three white T-shirts at a store named Target. Standing in front of a mirror at his sister's house dressed in his new clothes made him grin. He liked the brightness of his new tennis shoes and T-shirt, the dark blue of his brand-new jeans. But his smile, he suddenly noticed, wasn't like the orderly white smiles of the Americans. It was a jumble of crisscrossing, faintly yellow teeth. From that moment forward, except when he was drunk, Jesús's smile became a closed-lipped shadow of its former self.

TWO MONTHS HAD PASSED when a roofer named Rodriguez didn't show up for work one Monday morning.

"The *pinche* cops picked him up on Saturday night for driving drunk," a hot-shot roofer named Manuel told Don Pedro. "He's being sent back to Mexico."

"*¡Cabrones!*" said Don Pedro, whose skin was dark and leathery from years of working on roofs. Though Dwayne was the official jobsite supervisor, Don Pedro was *el jefe* to the roofers. Like their fathers back in Mexico, he had gray in his sideburns and doled out wise counsel and small loans to those who fell short before payday. Unlike Dwayne—who acted like a *pinche* gringo and whose Tidewater accent they couldn't understand anyway—Don Pedro had earned their respect. The guys actually listened to him.

"*Déjame hacerlo,*" Jesús begged Don Pedro. "I can do Rodriguez's job, I know how." For months, he had studied the roofers at work. How they rolled out the tar paper and tacked it down; how they carefully measured and snapped the lines of chalk; how they fit the gritty, dark gray shingles up to the line. How they held their oddly shaped hammers at just the right angle to drive in the short, flatheaded nails efficiently.

Don Pedro laughed and nodded at Jesús. "*Hazlo pues, hijo.*" Go for it, kid.

He and the other roofers thought it a great joke. They placed bets on how long the small, skinny kid from Guanajuato would last in the midday sun. But Jesús was agile and strong, like the howler monkeys of Oaxaca, and the men underestimated how smart and ambitious he was. He scrambled up the ladder and was soon working as fast, and with as much precision, as many of the more experienced guys. After that day, his wage jumped from six dollars to fifteen, sixteen, and on good days, seventeen dollars an hour.

JESÚS SENT NINE HUNDRED DOLLARS back to Mexico to retire the debt he still owed friends and relatives for his passage to the U.S. Every payday, he gave a little money to his sister to help with the mortgage and food. He supplemented his mother's meager income by wiring money to her each month. Soon he would have to send money to Lupita, too. A month after he'd left, she called to say she was expecting a baby in September. Still, the cash he had in his pockets felt hot, like the *comal* his mama cooked the family's tortillas on. He was earning ten times what he could in Mexico and soon forgot about his dream of saving for school. *Who needs to go to school when you can make so much money?* Jesús thought. *There is so much to buy in America!*

He began to envy the guys he worked with, especially the ones who'd been in the U.S. for years. They drove big cars and trucks and SUVs, rigs with souped-up sound systems, leather seats, and mag wheels. Jesús especially coveted the shiny red Dodge Ram truck with gleaming chrome rims Don Pedro drove. Unlike the younger workers, who preferred Nirvana and Pearl Jam, *el jefe* played *rancheras*, the songs of home, on his car stereo. Jesús couldn't afford a car, but he thought a stereo for his room at his sister's house would be nice. He too could play rancheras and Tejano tunes on it and dream of being back in Puerto de Nieto making love to Lupita.

ONE NIGHT IN EARLY JULY, Jesús saw an ad on TV for stereos at a store named Best Buy. The following Sunday, his one day off, he hopped on a local bus and went on his first solo shopping trip. In his meager English, Jesús managed to communicate to a salesman at Best Buy that he wanted to buy a stereo. "Well, you've come to the right place!" said the big, smiling, red-faced man who looked well-fed to Jesús. They spent a half hour studying the many options, each one a little more expensive than the last.

"You want the best, don't you?" the salesman kept asking Jesús, who had never owned the best of anything. The idea of owning one of the fancy black sound systems made him giddy and light-headed. Adrift on a sea of unrequited desire, he forgot about the rent he owed his sister. He forgot about how much his mother depended on the dollars he sent home. He forgot about Lupita and how she would soon need money for the child they were expecting. All he could think about was how beautiful the brand-new sound systems were.

An hour later, he was the owner of a massive new stereo with four booming speakers that the salesman would have delivered for free the very same day.

"Adiós, amigo!" the salesman said, pumping Jesús's square hand enthusiastically.

On the way home from the bus stop, Jesús began to feel uneasy about his purchase—how big it was, how much money it cost, how little money he had left to singe his fingers on. Mired in remorse, he didn't notice the four teenage boys following him until it was too late. One of them grabbed him by the collar and dragged him into an alley. The others punched and kicked and knocked him to the ground. "Motherfucking Mexican!" one yelled as he rifled Jesús's pockets for his few remaining dollars.

AT WORK ON MONDAY, the guys teased him about his swollen right eye and the purplish-yellow bruises on his cheek.

"¡Ay, Chuy! Looks like those *burros americanos* got ahold of you!" Manuel chided.

But Jesús ignored their ribbing and got to work. He was intent on earning back the money he'd lost as quickly as possible and was so focused he didn't notice when Dwayne—sporting the same mirrored aviator glasses as los federales, Mexico's much-hated federal police—drove up in his black Ford-250. Manuel switched from harassing Jesús to making fun of Dwayne under his breath.

"*Ojo, que ahí viene el tirano,*" he said, glaring at the tall, lanky tyrant, who climbed out of his truck and kicked a large clod of dirt out of the way with the tip of his boot.

"Manuel, Chuy, Paco, Tony, Pedro!" Dwayne shouted. "Y'all get on down here and hurry up 'bout it!"

Once the roofers were assembled, their supervisor stood in front of them with his arms crossed over his chest, which made him look even more like a *pinche* cop.

"The Prince William County Board of Supervisors don't want Mexicans working here no more," he said. "They took a vote last week sayin' it's illegal for you to work in this county, so y'all are gonna have to gather your stuff up and git off the property."

The guys stared at him, baffled by both his accent and his words.

But Don Pedro understood perfectly. In a measured voice, he translated what Dwayne had said, so all the roofers would also clearly understand.

"*¿Ahorita?*" Manuel asked.

"You mean right now?" Don Pedro translated for Dwayne.

"Yeah, I mean right now. Git goin'."

For once the guys had nothing to say. They stared at Dwayne in stunned silence.

"Y'all can try again next year," he said, shrugging and turning his back to them so he wouldn't have to meet their eyes. "Maybe this'll all blow over by then."

WORK OVER THE WHOLE OF PRINCE WILLIAM COUNTY dried up faster than ditch water in Mexico's high desert in the month of

May. With no way to pay the mortgage and other bills, Jesús's older sister and her husband lost their house and along with it, their life savings.

Don Pedro saw the layoff as a sign from God that it was time to retire and drove back to Jalisco where his wife and family had been awaiting his return for twenty years. Three years later, at the age of sixty-two, he would be dead from pancreatic cancer.

The rest of the guys scattered, some to Baltimore, a few further north to Pennsylvania, where they'd heard there were plenty of jobs and no anti-immigrant laws. Jesús and Manuel headed south to New Orleans where word had it la Huracán Katrina had created an abundance of jobs. But that place also proved a bust work-wise; Louisiana was as inundated with itinerant workers as it had once been with water.

EVENTUALLY JESÚS GAVE UP on America. Broke and empty-handed (the new stereo being far too expensive to ship), he hitched a ride back to Mexico where a year later, surrounded by friends and family, and with their two-year-old daughter toddling around the altar, he married his sweetheart Lupita in Puerto de Nieto's blue and white parochial church. They moved into the two-room concrete block house he'd built on his mother's *rancho* where, over the next five years, Lupita would give birth to three more girls.

❀ ❀ ❀

Ten years later, Jesús is still in Mexico hustling for backbreaking work that pays less than twenty dollars a day. When unable to find work or on Sundays, his one day off, he spends his time improving his simple concrete block house, which has electricity, but no indoor plumbing. Like his mother and stepfather, he and Lupita keep chickens and goats and tend a patch of corn and beans, but with five mouths to feed, electric and gas bills, hospitals and doctors to pay, shoes and clothing and medicine to buy, money is always in short supply.

Still, Jesús has not stopped dreaming. In fact, he now spends his days and his nights dreaming of two things: having a son and returning to America.

At La Mesa Grande

I AM DRINKING GREEN TEA and checking my email at La Mesa Grande one morning when a young couple comes in and sits down at the table across from mine. Tall and slender, sporting a long golden ponytail and a brown leather jacket, the young man possesses a pearly smile that would break your heart. His dark-haired girlfriend is petite and pretty and wears a colorfully embroidered Mexican peasant blouse, like one I wore when I attended art school at the Instituto Allende in 1973.

I sit, catching furtive glimpses of the young lovers talking and holding hands across the table as they wait for their breakfasts to arrive when, suddenly, I see my old college boyfriend and me, as we were back then. Young, in love—still untouched by all the heartbreak and disappointment the future would bring— holding hands across a different wooden table in a different San Miguel café many years ago. And I wonder...

Did some woman, on the far side of life, once glance at us with the same mixture of nostalgia and longing?

Dreaming of Paris

B ALBINA DREAMS of going to Paris and I dream of taking her there. I dream of walking down the city's broad boulevards and along the Seine, past the famous cafés of Saint-Germain-des-Prés and along the Rue St. André des Arts with the stout, gray-haired Mexican woman who has been my housekeeper for seventeen years. I imagine us crossing the Pont Neuf and standing in front of Notre Dame, marveling at its grandeur. We'd sit together in the cathedral's dim interior, shafts of blue light filtering through its famous stained-glass rosette, Bach's *Toccata and Fugue in D Minor* echoing through the nave.

I fantasize about taking Balbina to see the Eiffel Tower. Ever since she saw a television program on the great cities of the world a few years ago, she has dreamt of seeing Paris and its famous tower. I envision us wandering through the Champ de Mars in early evening in order to arrive just as the tower's five billion tiny lights flash on. Balbina, wrapped in her finest red *rebozo*, would be awestruck. *"¡Ay! Dios mío!"* she'd exclaim upon seeing the monument's glitzy light show and the enormous crowd clustered at its base. We would forego climbing the tower's seventeen hundred steps because we're both afraid of heights. Instead we'd hover over the tourist trinkets sold at the base and buy four small glow-in-the-dark towers, one for each of her daughters.

In my dreams I see us cruising down the Seine on a Bateau Mouche. Balbina has never been on a boat. I dream of leading her up the Daru Staircase in the great hall of the Louvre to see the Winged Victory of Samothrace. Walking through the cob-bled streets of Montmartre. Introducing her to simple, provincial French fare: crepes and *cidre doux* from Brittany or *cassoulet* from the Dordogne. We'd eat couscous at my favorite Algerian restaurant in St. Michel and steak-frites at Le Procope, on the narrow alley near Odeon, where Franklin, Jefferson, Voltaire, and Robespierre once dined. Balbina would like the steak but miss the spicy Serrano chiles and salsa verde she's so fond of.

Balbina would love the French sense of style, because in her heart, she is not a housekeeper. In her heart, she is an interior designer. She regularly rearranges the furniture, rugs, art, and decorative accessories at my house, always to better effect.

SEVENTEEN YEARS AGO, the previous owner of my home in San Miguel de Allende sold it to me with one condition: I keep Balbina Tovar on as my housekeeper. I'd never owned a home in Mexico before and it hadn't occurred to me that I wanted or needed a housekeeper. But Gary Fink insisted. I am forever grateful he did, because I can't imagine life at Casa Chepitos without Balbina. Over the years we've formed a deep bond; some days it takes her twice as long to clean the house because we spend so much time talking. Family issues, health issues, philosophy, politics, religion, our aging bodies: we discuss it all. Though illiterate, Balbina is thoughtful and wise and, unlike so many of my American friends and family, she is not constantly checking her cell phone as we talk.

IN MY HEART, I know Balbina and I will never visit Paris together. Not because we couldn't eventually finagle a passport and visa for her. Not because she's never been outside of San Miguel, or on an airplane, or in a city as large as Paris and would be afraid. Balbina is one of the most courageous women I know. She stood up to San Miguel's local government—something poor, middle-aged mestizo women in Mexico rarely do—by marching into their offices and demanding they take down the unauthorized photo of her granddaughter in a wheelchair, which they'd plastered on buildings around town to prove that local tax dollars helped local people.

Rage flowed into her mellow voice the day she explained to me how, for years, she'd petitioned San Miguel's government to give her the money for the special wheelchair her granddaughter needed. "We got that wheelchair with money from a federal program, not from the city!"

BALBINA WILL NEVER SEE PARIS because she is her family's North Star, the one her six children and husband steer by. Her sturdy shoulders bear the weight of all their sorrows, their triumphs, misfortunes, and miscalculations. Balbina will never see Paris because she is not only a primary breadwinner, she's also the main caregiver for her severely disabled fourteen-year-old granddaughter. Born with grave physical impairments, the girl can barely sit up, let alone walk on her own. She suffers from allergies, asthma, and seizures. Twice a week, Balbina takes her granddaughter on an eight-hour round-trip journey by bus from San Miguel to Irapuato for physical therapy sessions. The cost of this, plus the doctor's visits, medicine, and continuous hospitalizations have kept the family in a state of financial crisis for years.

Balbina and I will also never see Paris together because no matter how much I might want our bond to be something more, there is no getting around the fact that we are forever bound by certainties that separate us: our upbringings, our educations, our exposure to the world, and the significant financial disparity that exists between us. Though we may care deeply about each other, transcending these disparities is not something easily accomplished. Am I naïve—or maybe even patronizing—to imagine it could be otherwise?

BALBINA WILL NEVER SEE PARIS and that makes me sad. A few years ago, as a small consolation, I bought her a wall calendar of the City of Light with color photographs of the boulevards and quays, the churches and parks, the gardens and museums we will never visit together. I am well aware of what a small gesture it was, but I am also aware that sometimes small gestures are all we can do. I also know that, after ten years, those photographs of Paris are still pinned to her living room walls.

How to Write About
Your Mexican Housekeeper

1. Start with a descriptive scene steeped in sentimentality. Like the day she taught you how to make *salsa verde* or when she went out of her way to help you decorate the house for your sixty-fifth birthday party. Or maybe show the reader how she sweeps so efficiently and makes up the beds so perfectly. Describe how dependable she is and how her steadiness makes you feel secure in Mexico, a place that can often feel so insecure.

2. Make sure to describe your housekeeper as short, *mestiza*, gray-haired, and brown-skinned—these are obvious descriptors for a large portion of the female population in Mexico, and other expats (your audience) will know exactly who you are talking about. Also, make sure to mention that she has six or seven children and fourteen or more grandchildren even though she's ten years younger than you (who still have *no* grandchildren).

3. Consider referring to her as your maid, not your housekeeper. Housekeeper sounds too formal and kind of stuffy.

4. State what's at stake for your housekeeper, especially if it really has nothing to do with you. For instance, maybe she has a son who she's hoping can continue with his studies but he has no money to do so, or a daughter working in the U.S. who she fears will never be able to come home for a visit now that the *cabrón* Trump is president. Show how much these people

mean to you even though you've never met them. They are, after all, related to your poor, dear housekeeper.

5. Make sure to use at least one clichéd Mexican expression in every paragraph even if you don't have any idea what it means or how to spell it. Your readers, especially the ones who don't speak Spanish, will think this is very exotic.

6. Continue in this vein but add a few food-related details that every well-traveled reader can savor. Carry on about your housekeeper's deliciously spicy tortilla soup, her fluffy hand-made tortillas, or the colorful *chiles en nogada* she made for your Mexican Independence Day fiesta that you thought was celebrated on May 5th until she so generously corrected you.

7. Make sure to add some bit about your housekeeper's unrealized life and dreams or how desperately poor her family is in order to pull on your reader's heartstrings. But make sure *not* to mention how when you misplace a five-hundred-peso bill or lose a ring or necklace in your Mexican house you sometimes start to wonder…

8. Add a little background history: how she's been with you for sixteen years or how she came so highly recommended by friends or how desperately she needed the job, to let people know just how authentic your relationship is. Forego letting the reader in on your little secret: you really don't speak much Spanish and your housekeeper doesn't speak English at all. And how, half the time, you can only nod agreeably because you have no idea what she's talking about.

9. Cite an example of some terrible obstacle she faced early in life, like nearly starving to death in childhood or not owning a pair of shoes until she was twelve years old. Make sure to add the part about how much you admire her strength in the face

of all that adversity. Or conversely, talk about how much her simplicity and unquestioning nature inspire you to be a better person. DO NOT, however, tell your readers how you privately cringe at the thought of ever having to live a life like hers.

10. End the essay by referring back to something you did to help your housekeeper: how you gave her the money her son needed to attend that school or those almost-new shoes and clothes you were about to donate to the church tag sale. Or how about mentioning the calendar with the beautiful images of Paris you gave her after she told you she'd always dreamed of seeing the Eiffel Tower? Because what's really important is that your readers understand what a kind and generous person *you* are. Right?

The Lump

I MIGHT NEVER HAVE NOTICED the cat's-eye-sized lump just above my collarbone if it hadn't been for the mosquito that bit me right on top of it. Which is somewhat odd since mosquitos are rare in my Seattle neighborhood. We have more than our fair share of ants, yellow jackets, fleas, and fruit flies, but very few mosquitos. However, one found me, which led me to finding the lump.

And I might have ignored the lump if my older sister and several close friends hadn't all been diagnosed with thyroid cancer that year. Every month someone new seemed to be falling prey to the surgeon's knife. In my sister Margaret's case, the cancer had spread so extensively throughout her neck tissue it took the surgeon seven hours to remove it. At one point he came out to ask our ninety-three-year-old mother for permission to continue scraping the cancerous cells off of her vocal cords.

"There's a chance she'll lose her voice," he warned her. My mother implored him to cut out all the malignant cells, but I remember thinking at the time that it would be terrible if Margie lost her voice, because she might no longer be able to sing. She'd always had the prettiest voice of my three sisters.

SINGING TOGETHER is the most consistent bond my sisters and I share. For the four of us harmonizing is a soothing act, one that has held our large family together through good times and bad. I learned to sing almost as early as I learned to talk. The summer I was two years old my sister Frances, who was ten years my senior, went off to YMCA camp and came home with a repertoire of camp songs she immediately taught her younger sisters. "You Are My Sunshine" and "I Love the Daffodils" were the first of many songs we learned to harmonize on or sing in rounds. Later, we added Christmas songs, gospel tunes, and Broadway hits to our repertoire.

We were always singing. We sang in the car, we sang at summer camp, we sang at church, and during the holidays. We sang for birthday parties, weddings, and anniversaries. In high school and college, we taught ourselves to play guitars and learned the protest songs of Pete Seeger, Joan Baez, and Bob Dylan. When our brother died a senseless death at age fifty-four and we found ourselves at a loss for words, we circled his grave and sang.

❀   ❀   ❀

MY SISTER'S SEVEN-HOUR SURGERY and the prospect of my own lump being cancerous scared me enough to make an appointment with my doctor. At her office a week later, she asked how long it had been there. "I have no idea," I said. "I didn't notice it until a mosquito bit me right there." She palpated the lump and ordered an ultrasound.

At the radiology clinic, a rheumy-eyed Welsh technician kept clearing his throat and saying "uh-oh" as he pushed a Doppler wand in circles around my neck. This did not allay my fears. As I tried to lie perfectly still on the paper-covered table, he kept excusing himself and running from the room. The sixth or seventh time, I snuck a peek at the screen where I saw my neck tissue pulsating to the beat of my heart and noticed a large round dark mass. By the time the Welshman returned, I was imagining my own seven-hour surgery. I felt sheepish when he informed me that the suspicious dark mass was my carotid artery.

The radiologist who read the ultrasound emailed to ask what type of thyroid cancer my sister had. "Metastatic papillary thyroid carcinoma," I responded. Being papillary, not medullary, indicated that my lump was not genetically related to my sister's, but the doctor set a date for a needle biopsy anyway. The day before I left for San Miguel de Allende, Mexico, where I live for part of the fall and winter each year, a physician's assistant aspirated the lump with an enormous needle that looked like something you might use to inject an elephant. A few hours later, my neck broke out in hives. For weeks, thousands of tiny, itchy red bumps covered my throat and upper chest. I emailed my doctor from Mexico. She had no idea why it was happening but told me to apply a hydrocortisone cream and assured me that she would forward the biopsy results as soon as they arrived. Three weeks later the rash finally disappeared, and her email popped up in my inbox. The endocrinology department had labeled my biopsy report as "indeterminate." They recommended repeating the biopsy in two to three months.

As is my habit, I obsessed about the lump. I'd wake at three a.m. and in the darkness, my mind instantly began imagining the worst. During the day I could not keep my hands off of it. My fingers relentlessly searched it out, checking its size and shape and firmness. What if cancer was spreading through my neck? What if I too fell under the surgeon's knife? What if *I* lost my singing voice?

"Consider yourself lucky," my friend Muriel said. "Thyroid cancer is one of the 'good' cancers." I found her comment unhelpful. I didn't feel lucky. I felt anxious. I doubted there were any "good" kinds of cancer. It seemed to me there were bad cancers, worse cancers, and ones that kill you in six weeks or less.

I told Gracia and Lupe about the lump. When I told them my sister had had thyroid cancer and that I was afraid that I might too, they said they would pray for me. For some reason this felt more reassuring than anything else that I'd tried so far.

I SCHEDULED AN APPOINTMENT with Eduardo Morales, a cranial-sacral and polarity therapist at Life Path Center for the Healing Arts. The day we met, I explained that I was there because I needed to calm my growing hysteria about the lump and that I hoped a polarity treatment might help dispel some of my nervous energy. Eduardo mentioned in passing that, in addition to being a cranial-sacral and polarity therapist, he was also a *curandero*. A traditional Mexican healer. And that he came from Tepoztlán, the land of traditional Mexican healers.

Nothing he did or said during the treatment that day was indicative of any traditional or indigenous medical practice. No spells were cast or incantations said over my thyroid gland. He didn't prescribe herbs or burn incense. He didn't cover my neck with a salve made from peyote, as a Huichol curandero might. Yet, two days later, the lump mysteriously disappeared. I woke up one morning and when my fingers compulsively reached for it, it was gone. When I mentioned this to Gracia and Lupe, they weren't surprised. "We prayed to the Virgin of Guadalupe," Lupe said with a smile and a little shrug. "She made it go away."

I wondered if maybe it was the *milagros*, the tiny silver charms in the shapes of heads and torsos that Balbina had started placing around my bedroom after Gracia told her about the lump on my neck. The milagro board at the San Juan del Dios church in San Miguel is full of miniature silver hearts and heads, legs, arms and torsos, many of them attached to notes with healing prayers for the sick, the crippled, and the mentally imbalanced.

I'LL NEVER KNOW FOR SURE why the lump disappeared. I only know that it has been gone for two years now and shows no sign of coming back. I'm also happy to report that my sister's cancer is in remission and her voice has returned to normal. We are both still singing.

Machita

MACHITA, WITH HER wandering eye and toothless grin, chases dust around and around the alley as Lupe and I sit watching.

"She sweeps and sweeps but it never makes any difference!" Lupe says with a snicker.

Machita, with the mind of a five-year-old and a body sixty years older, has no family—no husband, no children, no sisters or brothers. No home and no one to care for her except the people who live along callejón Chepito. To earn money, she hauls our garbage to the corner three days a week or runs up and down the Cuesta de San José doing errands for Balbino's fat wife and a few other women who live on the alley.

With the pesos they pay her for running down the hill to buy their *jitomates* and tortillas, Machita purchases cheap plastic headbands at a stand in the market. Each week she sports a new one in her closely cropped gray hair. Today it is orange and pink striped; last week it was blue and green tie-dyed. Once she had a headband with bunny ears. *"La coneja,"* Gracia called her, until some boys on the callejón stole the headband and yanked the ears off.

Machita tilts her head to the side like a sparrow and babbles at whomever will listen to her in a garbled tongue I cannot understand. A language even Lupe and Gracia can't understand. She sits on the bench in front of my house or on the curb beneath the Cruz de San José, talking to herself or eating the tacos our neighbors give her and drinking Coca-Cola from small plastic cups.

MACHITA WAKES AT SIX A.M. on Monday, Wednesday, and Friday, dons her blue wool skirt and worn-out penny loafers, and drags the detritus of other people's lives down the alley to the corner where she hands off her black plastic burdens to boys who heave them atop the giant oozing piles that fill the backs of their trucks.

Though she's the one who hauls the garbage to the corner, it's Balbino who collects our money. In exchange, he lets her sleep on a *petate* mat on the floor at the back of his house. Then one day his wife kicks her out.

"She was waking everyone at four in the morning with her sweeping," Gracia explains. Balbino's wife told her to stop but Machita couldn't. Sweeping is her obsession.

I nearly trip over her early one morning in Gracia's kitchen. She's asleep on the cold tile floor beside the dining table. She has no mat, no sleeping bag, no blanket—only an old maroon sweater wrapped tightly around her.

"Señora Juana offered to let her sleep on the bed in her living room," Gracia says. But Machita refused.

When I look at her questioningly, Lupe whispers: "She was raped when she was young, and she hasn't slept in a bed since." An ache forms in my throat. I run across the alley to Casa Chepitos.

❀　❀　❀

AS I RUMMAGE THROUGH MY LINEN CLOSET for an old blanket to give Machita, I think about Seattle's growing homeless crisis. About the young and old men in sleeping bags I step over or around to get out of my apartment building or into the grocery store. The stooped and weatherworn women who push red Safeway carts loaded with their worldly possessions up and down Broadway. The lines of aged, frowning immigrants— Chinese, Vietnamese, Japanese, Polish—in front of the Jewish Federation Foodbank I pass each Friday morning on my way to Central Co-op to do my shopping. Of the guilt I feel passing them a second time with my sack full of carefully chosen groceries.

I think about how Seattle's annual homeless body count has quadrupled in the last five years; about the stray needles and people overdosing on the streets; the raging psychotics outside my window at three a.m.; the human feces I dodge while walking my dog in the morning; the tents filling parking strips and vacant lots and underpasses around the city; the spoiled food, filthy sleeping bags, and plastic water bottles spilling out of covered doorways; the tent cities and homeless encampments that have homeowners in those neighborhoods all riled up.

The more their numbers grow, the less capable we are of seeing the homeless as individuals. Individuals in need.

Instead we wring our hands, we argue about them at dinner parties, at City Council meetings, and on KUOW's *Week in Review*; we fund studies, vote to tax ourselves and visitors to help them and then use the money for other purposes—like tidying up Safeco Field for the Mariners, our equally hopeless baseball team. Meanwhile, Seattle's homeless situation worsens.

What we don't do: we don't invite the homeless to sleep in our extra rooms, use our bathrooms, or sit at our dining tables. That would be absurd, unthinkable.

❀ ❀ ❀

MACHITA DIED ON A COLD DAY in February and mass was held for her at San Miguel's Oratorio. Our homeless neighbor loved churches, especially the Oratorio. At special masses for the children, she was always there, sitting alone in the front row. On the day of her funeral mass my neighbors from callejón Chepito had packed every pew in the church and by the time I arrived there was nowhere left to sit. I stood at the back next to Julito, no longer the snotty-nosed kid who grew up with my kids, but a grown man with a full black mustache and two young daughters. The service was long and the priest said prayers for Machita I'd never heard in my fifteen years in San Miguel. When I quietly questioned Julito about it, he told me the priest was honoring her with a special mass.

"Maybe because Machita was so faithful," he said with a small shrug. "Or maybe because God was the only real family she had."

*   *   *

THE LAST TIME I SAW MACHITA, I was up on my third-floor terrace. It was late afternoon and a blood-orange sun was slowly sinking behind the shadowy gray-green hills of the Santa Rosa mountains. Machita was leaning against the wall of Gracia's terrace—little more than three meters from me. Her chin rested on her arms as if she were deep in thought. For once, I thought, she's not in motion. She isn't manically sweeping, talking to herself, or gesticulating wildly.

Watching her, I couldn't help but wonder what she was thinking about. Was her childlike mind capable of reflection or regret? Of dwelling on all the sorrow she's suffered in this life? Did she worry about the future, as I would if I didn't have a husband and children who loved me or the financial security that I too often take for granted?

As I stood there on my terrace, wondering what she was thinking, Machita spotted me across the alley and lifted her hand in a little wave. Then she said in the clearest Spanish, without a hint of coyness or confusion or the bird-like tilt of her head: "Isn't it a beautiful afternoon, Señora?"

"*Sí, Machita,*" I said. It was all I could think of to say.

PART II ❀ VIAJES

Lucile and Warren Gille visiting ruins

The real voyage of discovery consists not in seeking new landscapes but in having new eyes.
— Marcel Proust

Ixchel & the Fertility Goddesses: From A to Z

*A*FRICANS, AZTECS, AUSTRALIAN *Aboriginals.* Every ancient culture had a fertility goddess and some had several. In ancient Egypt, Hathor and Isis personified joy, love, fertility, and motherhood; Hera, Artemis, and Rhea represented fertility, childbirth, and motherhood to the ancient Greeks; in Hindu mythology, Durga is the divine Mother Goddess, served by her goddess handmaidens Chandra, Parvati, and Sinivali.

Bamboozled. My first trip to Mexico was to the Yucatán Península in 1967. I was fourteen years old. My mother was studying cultural anthropology at the University of Missouri at Kansas City and thought it a "marvelous" idea to drag her three teenage daughters, neurotic husband, and clueless eight-year-old son to the Yucatán to traipse around ancient ruins in August, the hottest, most humid month of the year in Mexico. We couldn't have agreed less.

Celtic Goddess. The Celts worshipped the goddess Brig in pre-Christian Ireland. Brig, who later morphed into Saint Brigid after Catholicism firmly planted its roots on the Emerald Isle, represented fertility, motherhood, healing, and poetry. Brig lives on in the Feast of Saint Brigid, which marks the beginning of spring for the Irish.

DC-3. We flew from New Orleans to Mérida on a DC-3. Two distinct memories from that flight: the deafening roar of the plane's propellers and how my father's frown turned to a look of utter terror when he realized we were going to land in the middle of the jungle on an unpaved runway. Unlike his forefathers who navigated the Mississippi and explored great swathes of Canada and the U.S., there was not a single drop of adventurer in my father's French blood. When the pilot missed the runway on his first pass, Daddy—nearly apoplectic by then—said in an embarrassingly loud voice, "What the hell have you gotten us into, Lucile?"

(Big) Easy. Our itinerary for the trip to Mexico included a brief stopover in New Orleans. We spent our first night on Bourbon Street where my mother, busy chasing drunken men away from my sisters and me, lost track of my younger brother. We eventually found him inside a saloon, staring drop-jawed at a woman dancing on a rickety wooden bar, her barely clad body wrapped around a brass pole. Twelve years later my brother would return to New Orleans to attend Tulane University's School of Architecture and never leave the Big Easy again.

Fertility Goddesses. Across cultures these goddesses personify nature, fertility, childbirth, motherhood, the moon, medicinal plants, creation, and sometimes, destruction. They are associated with springtime, flowers, sex, and snakes.

Gaia. Gaia was a primal Greek goddess, the one who gave birth to the Titans. She was the original Mother Earth, but not specifically known as a fertility goddess in the Greek pantheon. Rhea and Artemis were fertility goddesses and two of Zeus's personal favorites. I once had a cat named Artemis Boo Radley.

Hotel Hacienda Mérida. My mother booked rooms for us at the Hotel Mérida, a charming colonial hotel with large rooms and a small swimming pool where my older sisters showed off their diving prowess for a couple of easily impressed AeroMéxico pilots. I was more interested in the hotel's bar, where they seemed happy to serve me as much tepid Coca-Cola and as many crunchy, fried Mexican snacks, which they called *botanas,* as I could eat and drink. All they needed was my room number!

Incan Goddesses. Mama Killa and Mama Ocllo were associated with the moon, menstrual cycles, and fertility and served as protectors to ancient Peruvian women.

Jungle Jaunt. Before leaving home, Mother contracted with a tour service in Mérida to have a guide accompany us on our weeklong excursion to the peninsula's archaeological sites deep in the jungle. She has always claimed that the tour company owner, a man named Felipe Escalante, originally intended for his nineteen-year-old nephew to act as our guide. But when he got a look at my petite, pretty, blonde-haired, blue-eyed mother and her three nubile teenage daughters, he decided that wasn't such a good idea. "It will be an enormous sacrifice," Señor Escalante told my mother, "but I, myself, will accompany you." Thus began our jaunt through the jungles of the Yucatán.

Killer Pyramid. We toured ruins at Chichén Itzá and Uxmal with Señor Escalante. The day we visited Chichén Itzá, the sacred site of the ancient Maya, it was devoid of visitors, except for one other family and a handful of French archaeologists working on an excavation at the Temple of the Warriors. Fewer than a thousand people visited Chichén Itzá annually in the 1960s and many of them were archaeologists, or students of Mayan culture, like my mother. While Daddy sat below and complained he couldn't breathe because of the "goddamn" heat and humidity, my sisters and I scrambled up the ninety-one steps of the massive pyramid known as El Castillo. The pyramid steps remained open to tourists until 2006 when an eighty-year-old woman from San Diego was killed in a fall.

Lectures. We clowned around on the ancient ball court and at the Temple of Warriors, and stared in horror at the Wall of Skulls, but the ancient ruins had about the same effect on us as visiting a ghost town in central Kansas. Mother tried to impress us with its cultural significance by delivering short pithy lectures. "At the height of Mayan civilization, tens, if not hundreds, of thousands of people lived here," she said. "Chichén Itzá was one of the most scientifically advanced cities in Mesoamérica." My sisters and I shrugged.

Mamá or Mamacita? As I remember it, Señor Escalante referred to my mother as *mamá*. She insists he called her *mamacita*. At Chichén Itzá there was a large hole in the ground with a shallow pool of murky green water at the bottom. "It's called the Cenote Sagrado," explained Señor Escalante. "They used to throw young virgins into it a long time ago." He threatened to throw my sisters Rachel and Margaret and me into the *cenote* "if we didn't listen to mamá."

No Way! I remember Señor Escalante also telling the three of us to rub the belly of a strange-looking stone figure with large breasts and stomach, a beak-like nose, and a snake for a headdress. When we asked who the strange figure was and what it represented, he said: "If you want to have children, you must rub her belly." "No way!" my sister Rachel said, recoiling. "I'm not touching that thing!" But Margaret and I happily rubbed the figure's belly. Even then we both knew we wanted to have children.

Ovulation. The figure, whose belly we were so anxious to stroke, was Ixchel, the ancient Mayan goddess of motherhood, the moon, ovulation, menstrual cycles, and medicinal plants. An earthly goddess who represented fertility and fecundity, Ixchel, not surprisingly, was also associated with bodies of water, rain, and tempests. According to a few goddess-worshipping websites, she's sometimes referred to as Lady Rainbow.

Pisté. On a recent trip to Kansas to visit my mother—now an ancient herself—we reminisced about that trip to the Yucatán. She remembered dancing with Señor Escalante in the dining room of our motel in Pisté and told me that Daddy threw a hissy fit that night. She said my father needled her about that inno- cent two-step until the day he died. Who knew Señor Escalante possessed such power?

Q'uq'umatz. The feathered snake god and creator Q'uq'umatz of the K'iche' Maya is closely related to the Yucatecán god Kukulcán, and to Quetzalcoatl, the most important god in the Nahua (Aztec) pantheon. In K'iche' Mayan mythology, Q'uq'umatz, along with the god Tepeu, was responsible for the creation of mankind. Like my father, Q'uq'umatz was a jealous guy, and one who could wreak havoc on the Maya if they annoyed him.

Ramón. Our family's last stop on that vacation was Isla Mujeres. When Francisco Hernández de Córdoba and his boat- load of Spaniards landed there in 1517, they found the island dotted with stone figures—all of them female. From that time forward the island has been known as the Island of Women. The stone figures the Spaniards encountered were Ixchel: the island was sacred ground for worshippers of the Mayan fertility goddess. I don't remember seeing any stone figures of Ixchel on our visit to Isla Mujeres. What I remember is being enchanted by the island's sea glass-colored waters; our simple whitewashed beach hotel with its mahogany shutters and ceiling fan; and a sweet-natured, brown-skinned boy named Ramón, who took my sisters and me out on his boat one day to swim with giant tortoises and eat fresh conch right out of the shell.

Sons. My sister Margaret, who is five years my senior, gave birth to two sons, the first in 1978 and the second in 1980. Rachel, the sister who refused to touch the figure of Ixchel, never did have children. Fifteen years after that trip to the Yucatán, my partner Paul and I managed to conceive the first month we tried, but then I miscarried ten weeks later. After waiting three months, per the doctor's orders, we started trying again. Nothing happened. Months went by with no luck. Each month my period came, I wanted to cry or scream. When a full year went by and there was still no sign of a baby on the horizon, I went to see an ob-gyn at Group Health Cooperative. "You're infertile," she announced matter-of-factly. "You'll probably never get pregnant again." I ignored her dire prediction and went to see a fertility specialist at UW Medicine. Dr. Moore couldn't find anything wrong. My fallopian tubes were open; my uterus was normally shaped and fully functional. I ovulated every month and my eggs were healthy. He ran tests on Paul's sperm and couldn't find a problem there either.

Talk, Talk, Talk. When you are unable to conceive, it's hard not to talk about it with anyone who will listen. If you've had the misfortune of miscarrying, getting pregnant again can become an obsession. While I was lamenting my infertility with a co-worker one day, she suddenly smiled and said, "I've got just the thing for you." The next day, she brought in a rustic clay figure, the kind of tacky trinket you might pick up at a tourist trap in Mexico. But it had familiar-looking breasts, stomach, and nose, the flat forehead of Mayan royalty, and a funny-looking crown. Ixchel!

Unbroken. I kept the clay icon by the side of my bed at night. I carried her around in my pocket by day. I rubbed her belly regularly. Three months later, on a full moon night in June, I finally got pregnant again. Nine months and two days later my water broke at 6 a.m. on International Women's Day and my son was born at 4:38 a.m. the next morning. A short time later, when another friend confided she was having a hard time getting pregnant, I gave her the figure of Ixchel. Within a few months, she too was pregnant. My friend passed the clay figure on to someone else. I hope that person got pregnant, too, and passed it on to someone else in need of a little goddess magic. May Ixchel's power to produce miracles remain unbroken.

Vanished. In 1967 a handful of *chicleros* were still harvest-ing *chicle* (the natural latex once used to make chewing gum) from sapodilla trees in the Yucatán. Outside of Mérida, the Maya spoke more Yucatec than Spanish, lived in grass-roofed huts with dirt floors, and slept in hammocks. According to my now ninety-eight-year-old mother, Cancún was nothing but a long narrow strip of white sand with one large, lonely backhoe parked there the day we passed it on our way to Puerto Juárez where we caught a boat to Isla Mujeres.

Mérida is now a bustling, cosmopolitan city with dozens of luxury hotels, a sweeping *malecón*, and a large expat community. Chicle has been replaced by synthetic gum and far fewer Maya sleep in hammocks in grass-roofed huts. But the changes to the area's sacred Mayan sites are the most radical of all. Chichén Itzá, now a UNESCO World Heritage site, hosts more than 1.4 million tourists annually. Busloads of people are dumped there each morning, and at night, a light-and-sound spectacle brings even more tourists to watch as its carved stone walls are flooded with colored lights and 3-D warriors while hokey music and the voices of "spirits" boom from giant speakers making me wonder: is the sacredness of the site as vanished as the ancient civilization itself?

Woman Falls from the Sky. In North America, an Iroquois origination legend has it that Ataensic (also known as Sky Woman) was unjustly cast out of heaven by her husband. However, as she fell from the sky, a flock of water birds rescued her and carried her on their wings to a great hole filled with water. A giant tortoise emerged from the water and Ataensic made his back her home and called it Turtle Island. I sometimes wonder if my curious, culture-and-nature-loving mother might also have fallen from the sky.

Xōchiquetzal. Goddesses and goddess worship were plentiful throughout pre-Columbian cultures. In Mexico, Aztec women worshipped Xōchiquetzal, whose name is derived from the word *xōchitl* (birth) and *quetzalli* (precious feather) in Náhuatl. Cempazúchil (marigolds) were sacred to this goddess, who gave birth to the god Quetzalcoatl, and birds and butterflies followed Xōchiquetzal wherever she went. Dogs, cats, rabbits, roosters, birds, even bees were attracted to my mother (I once watched her pet a bumble bee).

Younger Brother. One of Ixchel's many traits is that she can be very temperamental. When she's in a good mood she brings gentle rains so the earth can flourish, but when she's angry she unleashes her wrath in the form of floods and hurricanes. My younger brother—the one who moved to New Orleans forty years ago—had his own run-in with the goddess Ixchel in late August 2005 when much of his beloved city was inundated by a femme fatale named Katrina.

Zenith. From the *Merriam-Webster* dictionary: 1. the highest point on the celestial sphere vertically above a given position or observer. 2. a highest point or state; culmination.

It will be fifty years this summer since my family and I first visited the Yucatán's Mayan ruins. My father died on the eve of my mother's seventy-third birthday in 1992. In the twenty-seven intervening years, her fascination with indigenous cultures only grew. After Daddy passed, my mother continued to travel, unimpeded, to archaeological sites all over the world.

For the last eighteen years I've lived part-time in San Miguel de Allende. Like my mother, I've become an avid student of ancient Mexico, its history, culture, and art, and I'm drawn to the idea of returning to Chichén Itzá during the spring or fall equinox when the late afternoon sun creates an image of a snake creeping down the northern staircase of El Castillo. According to my friend Eduardo, it is an extraordinary thing to witness. The shadow, he says, is the feathered serpent god Kukulcán who, for a few fleeting moments, returns to join heaven and earth and the underworld, the darkness and the light, together.

The Trip to Taninul

THE SUMMER OF 2008 in Mexico brought weather akin to monsoon season in South Asia. The rains arrived early in June and came down in great sheets. Water ran, ankle-deep, in the callejón for an hour every day and our downstairs, below-grade bathroom flooded almost daily. San Miguel's dusty soil quickly became saturated and the town's streets waterlogged. Day after day, we woke to dark skies filled with clouds that brought ever more rain. Massive flooding and landslides were displacing thousands of people in coastal areas in Mexico, but my family and I remained naively unaware of the extent of the flooding in other parts of Mexico because we weren't in the habit of watching local news at Casa Chepitos. Instead we tuned into the BBC, a news program everyone could comprehend, and the channel that provided the world news my husband, Paul, prefers. This was our first mistake.

Of course, that was also the summer cousin Jake and his family returned for their second visit to Casa Chepitos, and like a band of fools, we decided that traveling halfway across Central Mexico in search of a sun that had gone AWOL in San Miguel was a good idea. This was the second in what would turn out to be a long chain of errors.

IT ALL STARTED BECAUSE Laura and Andy, Jake's mom and dad, had booked rooms at the Hotel Taninul, a hot spring resort located in an area around Tampico known as the Huasteca (a place where the red-hot, pulsating music of the same name originated). In pre-Columbian times, Huastecan royalty supposedly bathed in the mineral-rich pools at Taninul for health reasons. The hotel's website even advertised the thermal baths "as a cue for a multitude of symptoms including arthritis, rheumatism, skin problems and aging" and claimed that the same spa experience, once enjoyed by pre-Columbian royalty, was now available to lowly commoners like us.

Paul and I thought spending a few days at the coast, far away from our flooding bathroom and leaky skylight, sounded like a good idea. Sitting in thermal pools, being cured of our "aging" had its appeal. Plus, we wanted more time with cousin Jake and his family. So, we called the hotel's reception, booked a room for three nights, then ran to the bank to wire the required deposit to secure the room for our arrival the next day. That night we went online to study the hotel's website.

Among the enticing photos of waterfalls and reposing, blonde-haired women indulging in massage treatments, we found an advertisement for facial treatments made from "scum" gleaned from the sides and bottoms of the pools. I'm a great fan of mistranslations. My daughter Hannah and I amuse ourselves by cruising the shelves of Uwajimaya, our local Asian food emporium, for creatively translated advertising copy. Among our favorites is a slogan on the Milkis-brand Korean soda which reads "New feeling of soda beverage!"

We all chuckled at the notion of treating our skin with pool "scum," but it never occurred to any of us that a few such communication lapses would turn our weekend trip to Taninul into the journey from hell.

THAT NIGHT WE ALSO PULLED OUT our Guía Roji map of Mexico and discovered there was no direct way of getting to the Gulf Coast from San Miguel. One choice was to head over to Highway 57, take it northwest for nearly 200 kilometers to San Luis Potosí, and then turn east at Highway 70. These roads are federal highways, meaning they're well maintained, but the tolls are expensive and tollbooths ubiquitous. In some places, they're only a few hundred yards apart.

The other option was to drive south past Querétaro to San Juan del Río where you pick up Highway 120, a two-lane highway that twists and turns for 300 kilometers through Mexico's Sierra Gorda mountains.

We settled on the former, straighter route over better highways and started out early the next morning, for the five-to-six-hour drive. With a stop for lunch, maybe seven. Paul and I rented the last car available at the Hola Rent-a-Car in San Miguel: a late model Nissan with no air-conditioning and malfunctioning seatbelts. Andy and Laura and their kids were just ahead of us, in their own car.

The 200 kilometers to San Luis Potosí was an easy drive for our small caravan. Paul intently tailed Andy, who not only speaks fluent Spanish, but also had the directions to the hotel. We only missed one turn and quickly got back on track, arriving at Highway 70 around 11:00 a.m. as planned. This was where we would head east toward Río Verde and the Huasteca. At the juncture of the two highways we came to the fourth toll-booth of the still-young day and paid a usurious fee of 160 pesos (*mordidas,* the bribes tourists often pay to appease police in Mexico, can be less costly than the highway tolls). Just beyond the tollbooth was a rest stop where we took a lunch break at a Subway, then we got back on the highway.

Less than five miles down the road, we came to a roadblock with signs indicating that the road was closed. None of us had noticed that there were no cars arriving from the opposite direction. The operator at the last tollbooth had said nothing. We looked on our map and realized that just north of us was a place called the Valle de los Fantasmas or Valley of the Ghosts. A perfect name for a place as silent and barren as this. We turned around and headed to a small nondescript beige building we'd seen a few hundred yards back that appeared to be a deserted security station.

Paul pulled into the parking lot, next to a white camper van with Texas license plates. A Mexican-American family was milling about next to it. I was barely out of the car before being accosted by a chubby eleven-year-old boy and his little sister, who was dressed head-to-toe in Hello Kitty garb.

"Where are you from?" he asked me in English.

"San Miguel de Allende," I told him.

He screwed up his face, as if I'd told him a really bad joke.

"I mean where are you really from?"

"Okay, we're from Seattle in the state of Washington. Where are you from?"

"I'm from San Antonio, in Texas." He then proceeded to fill me in on the details of his family's trip, all of the stops they'd made along the way, the sights they'd seen, which grandparents they were visiting and where those grandparents lived in Mexico. To my relief the flashing red lights of an approaching police car arrested the kid's travel narrative.

I HAD TO WORK HARD to squelch my urge to laugh when the sheriff for the state of San Luis Potosí stepped out of his patrol car. Never, in all of my rebellious years when friends and I referred to cops as pigs, had I run across a police officer who looked so porcine. He had the same smooth skin, beady dark eyes, and flat snout as a prize-winning pig I'd once seen at the San Juan county fair. His large round belly draped over the belt of the drab brown uniform state sheriffs across North America seem to wear. His jowls jiggled as he began speaking to the small group of tourists gathered in the parking lot.

"He says the road to Río Verde is closed because of flooding!" the young raconteur from San Antonio announced, assuming I needed him to translate. My brother-in-law Andy and his wife Laura stepped in and the three of us had a long conversation in Spanish with the sheriff, who turned out to be an extremely helpful and pleasant guy. Meanwhile my new friend from San

Antonio stood quietly at my side, deflated by the knowledge that we didn't need his translation services.

The sheriff recommended we return to the tollbooth, then continue north toward Monterrey until we reached Highway 75, where yet another pay-as-you-go road would take us into Río Verde. He couldn't tell us what the road conditions were like beyond that. Andy and Laura were determined to continue since they'd already paid for five days at the Hotel Taninul. Paul and I debated whether we should continue on or return to San Miguel. The fact that we also had wired money for three night's accommodations clinched our decision. I've learned from experience that deposit money in Mexico is almost never refundable. Hence, the seven of us soldiered on.

FROM THERE THINGS WENT FROM BAD TO WORSE. We wasted a half hour at the tollbooth while Andy unsuccessfully tried to convince an immovable toll collector that we shouldn't have to pay again since they neglected to tell us the road ahead was closed in the first place. Two hours later we arrived in Río Verde, a town we'd imagined as lush and verdant given its name, only to be disappointed by the dismal, working class town where road construction clogged nearly every street. We lost Andy and Laura when Paul mistakenly followed a car that looked like theirs down a side road. We circled around the town for forty minutes looking for them and finally gave up and stopped for gas at a Pemex. When we pulled up to the pump, there was Cousin Jake! His family just happened to be parked at the opposite pump.

It turned out that the highway between Río Verde and Ciudad Valles was also closed due to flooding, so we were forced to take Highway 80 south through the Sierra Gorda. By then it was already midafternoon. We'd been on the road for more than seven hours. We consulted various guidebooks and decided to stop in Jalpan for the night. We figured it would be another six-to-eight-hour ride along this winding road to reach the Hotel Taninul.

The vistas along Highway 80 were stunning and the mountains lush and verdant, but the road itself was narrow and full of switchbacks and S-curves. It slices through thickly treed mountainsides and back down into dense green river valleys lined with giant willow and Montezuma cypress. Evidence of recent flooding was everywhere. Silt and mud washed over the highway in the lower areas. Organic debris was mixed with the usual inorganic detritus one sees scattered across the countryside in Mexico. Several houses close along the river leaned at unusual angles, or had been swept downstream. The only thing encouraging us to keep going was that trucks and cars were arriving from the opposite direction.

DUE TO THE CURVES, TRAFFIC, AND BACKHOES blocking the road, it took us four hours to drive the 106 kilometers between Río Verde and Jalpan. At least Jalpan was a pleasant surprise, with sumptuous mountain views and a lovely central plaza. We checked into the Hotel Misión Jalpan and while the kids swam in the pool, I wandered over to see the first mission church built by Father Junípero Serra, a priest whose eighteenth-century development ambitions rivaled those of Donald Trump today. Father Serra went on from Jalpan to build thirty-five more mission churches across Mexico and California, but the priest's business tactics—not unlike the Donald's—included the systematic oppression of his peons. Some say Serra used brutal techniques to subjugate and enslave indigenous Mexicans and Native Americans. There was a great uproar among indigenous Mexicans and academics when Pope John Paul II proposed beatifying Father Serra in 1988. But in 2015, despite past protests by Native Americans and Mexicans, Pope Francis canonized Father Serra at the Basílica of the National Shrine in Washington.

"Father Serra sought to defend the dignity of the native community, to protect it from those who had mistreated and abused it," Pope Francis said to the 25,000 people gathered for the canonization mass.

I stood in front of a statue of Serra that faced our hotel, wondering if it was possible to create a true narrative about Mexico's complicated colonial past. How does one rationalize the fact that 90 percent of indigenous populations in California and Mexico were wiped out by disease and abuse after the arrival of the Spaniards and their Catholic missionary priests?

AFTER DINNER THE KIDS COMPLAINED of feeling ill. Hannah and I went back to our room where she threw up for the next two hours. When we awoke in the morning, she was better but I was exhausted from being up all night. I went down the street and stocked up on Gatorade at the local *tienda* and we hit the road once again.

The road we were traveling on passed through Xilitla (pro-nounced hee-*leet*-la). The town itself had nothing particular to recommend it, but several kilometers beyond it was one of the more surreal spectacles I've seen in Mexico: a sculpture garden called Las Pozas. A landscaper friend had once told me that this garden, created in the middle of the tropical rainforest of the Sierra Gorda by an eccentric Englishman named Edward James, was not to be missed. James, a huge collector of Surrealist art before coming to Mexico, bought up a large tract of mountain-side land and began creating his own bizarre and monolithic art forms in the dense jungle near Xilitla.

Paul, who was not enthusiastic about the idea of stop-ping and refused to pay the admission, sat, sweat-soaked and grumpy, at the entrance while I dashed through the expansive tropical garden. I climbed hundreds of narrow, moss-slicked steps through the deep-green jumble of overgrown houseplants. Around every bend, I came upon another strange, outrageously oversized sculpture, each more madcap than the last. Wild organic columns jutting skyward; cascading concrete arches; stairways leading to nowhere; fantastic flower sculptures, painted in wild pinks and eye-popping purples, putrid yellows and acid greens.

The main attraction—where I found Jake and his family— were the giant waterfalls in the middle of Las Pozas. People lined the narrow walkways, enjoying the cool mist and watching dozens of daredevil kids slide down treacherous, rocky embankments. Though the falls looked extremely dangerous, there were no keep-off or warnings signs posted as there would have been in the U.S. The reason for this is simple: in Mexico people don't litigate like we do in the U.S. When accidents happen they don't immediately look for someone else to blame or sue.

No one we asked knew what the road conditions were like beyond Xilitla. We learned that only the day before the road had been impassable, but cars and trucks seemed to be coming from the direction we were headed, so we got back into the cars and drove onward. Along the narrow, winding road we passed yet more bulldozers and backhoes clearing giant piles of mud and debris and downed trees off the road. Evidence that Mexico had moved into the new century.

The drive went slower than we'd hoped and we cheered when we finally reached Ciudad Valles. That city, like Río Verde, was unremarkable except for the oppressive heat and humidity. Even with every window rolled down, the interior of the Nissan felt like the inside of an oven. We drove straight through Ciudad Valles, desperate to get beyond the steaming city and on to the Hotel Taninul where we would cool off in the mineral-rich pools. "I need to soak away the ten years I've added on this trip!" I said to Paul.

The hotel turned out to be located in an area that, at least in the rainy season, is a mosquito-infested lowland. Even worse: we discovered that the hotel grounds were flooded and had been all week. The gardens, the grounds, the patios, and pools were awash in knee-deep, greenish-brown water with rafts of the miraculous facial scum floating in it.

Paul and I went in and found Andy and another newly arrived guest—a neatly dressed American who looked like he might be a retired military officer—attempting to converse with the receptionist who understood little English. The man wanted to know why no one had mentioned that the hotel grounds were underwater before he arrived and Andy questioned the clerk in Spanish. She shrugged and said she had no idea. He interpreted her response for the American who pressed Andy to demand a better response. She said she would ask the manager.

"Why can't these people just get their act together?" the American said, clearly steamed. The scene is one I often encounter in my travels south of the border.

❋ ❋ ❋

PRACTICALLY ANYONE WHO HAS EVER TRAVELED in Mexico will know what I am talking about when I say there exists a cultural gap between Americans and Mexicans that can affect communication, even when language is not a barrier and the best intentions are at work. The reason for this is the profoundly different psychological makeups of Americans and Mexicans.

Americans still believe, on a nearly cellular level, in the concept of Manifest Destiny. While we no longer openly say aloud that God's will is what drives us to dominate the world, when we are abroad, we often act as though our way of thinking and doing things is how things *should* be done. Not only is our way best for us, but it's best for the rest of the world, too. That's why judging others, offering opinions, and giving advice comes so naturally to many Americans. And why we pose the question of why people in other cultures "just can't get their act together."

Mexicans, on the other hand, believe it's impolite to tell others what to do or how to do it. Being courteous, patient, and observant of rules or regulations are principles they adhere to fairly strictly. They are also fatalistic and resigned to the suffering this human life is bound to serve up. They see this as a normal part of living. To the Mexican way of thinking life brings problems, problems bring suffering, and suffering brings a sense of resignation. This is especially true among Mexico's poor and working-classes. According to Octavio Paz, resignation is one of Mexico's noblest virtues. "We admire fortitude in the face of adversity more than the most brilliant triumph," he wrote in *The Labyrinth of Solitude*. The antithesis of the American view.

         ❁   ❁   ❁

BEING EXHAUSTED FROM TWO DAYS OF DRIVING, we decided to stay at the Hotel Taninul, despite it being flooded. But even that was a mistake. Laura contracted salmonella from something she ate in the dining room that evening and by the next morning she was violently ill. Evidently, she wasn't alone. The doctor who treated her, who was also a guest at the hotel, told us he had treated several other hotel guests for salmonella.

While Andy rushed off to Ciudad Valles in search of antibiotics for Laura, Paul and Hannah and I packed our bags. After a long conversation with the hotel's manager, I did manage to get our third night refunded. It was noon by the time Andy returned and so hot you could have fried an egg on the Nissan's hood. But all I wanted was to get home to Casa Chepitos, so we left in the midday heat.

The ride back was nearly as bad as the ride there. We drove two hours out of our way when we were mistakenly informed that the road between Ciudad Valles and Río Verde had been reopened, which it was not. We were forced to take a detour north instead of heading south toward San Miguel. We were halfway to Monterrey before we were able to turn south again toward the state of Guanajuato and home.

The heat in the front seat was so intense I nearly passed out. Hannah was knocked out from the Dramamine I'd given her for car sickness, so we spent the entire afternoon slumped in the back seat together, while Paul, a real hero on that trip, just kept driving.

BY LATE AFTERNOON our supply of bottled water was long gone and we were desperate to find more. But it was Sunday, and late on a Sunday afternoon in that very rural part of Mexico, no stores were open. We drove through dusty village after dusty village where stray dogs roamed in deserted school yards, but all of the tiendas were closed.

We were desperately thirsty when we drove into a verdant valley, where gently undulating green hills were dotted with grazing cattle. Looming in the distance, Paul spotted a bright-white building.

"It says Kansas on the side," he said.

"Are you hallucinating?" I asked from my prone position in back.

"No, really. It says Mini-Super Kansas."

I sat up and saw a tidy, square concrete block building with MINI-SUPER KANSAS stenciled across the side in bold black letters. Our oasis in the Sahara.

"Stop!" I shouted. "It's open!"

THE MINI-SUPER KANSAS turned out to be like no other convenience store I've ever visited, before or since, in the middle of rural Mexico. For starters, it was air-conditioned. Second, the place was so clean that I felt like lying down on the tidy smooth-tiled floors and going to sleep. Third, the proprietor, a young mother with a toddler straddled on her hip, was as pretty as Salma Hayek. Alongside the coolers full of Coca-Cola, she stocked Arizona Tea, Vitamin Water, and Evian. I bought US$20 worth of drinks and snacks and suspected it was her biggest sale of the day.

On the way out, I couldn't help asking a pleasant-looking man in a short-sleeved plaid shirt, sipping a Coke outside the store, if he knew how it came to be named Kansas. "My wife and I lived in western Kansas for nine years. We love it there. We'd go back in a minute if I could get a green card," he said in nearly perfect English.

"I grew up in Kansas," I told him. What I didn't tell him was that, unlike he and his wife, I couldn't wait to leave Kansas. At age eighteen I left for college on the East Coast and have never looked back. I figured it was all a matter of perspective.

IT WAS AFTER TEN O'CLOCK by the time we arrived back at Casa Chepitos. It was a clear, starlit night in San Miguel and it took only a few minutes for the fresh evening air to revive our spirits and calm our exhausted, overheated bodies. When we opened the door onto our house's cool, luxuriant courtyard garden, I can honestly say that being home again had never felt so good. As I said, it's all a matter of perspective.

A Visit to Casa Trotsky

I FIRST MET my father-in-law in 1981 when my then-boyfriend Paul and I traveled to Texas to see his grandfather, who'd been diagnosed with cancer. As we climbed out of a rental car in Houston's Meyerland neighborhood, Paul's dad crossed the front lawn to meet us. But as he approached the car, he didn't look at us or extend any words of welcome to me or to Paul, who hadn't seen his father for nearly seven years. Instead he glanced sideways at his son as if he wasn't quite sure who he was and after an awkward moment said: "Hello Paul. Would you like to see my fruit trees?"

A child prodigy born to Jewish intellectuals in 1921, my father-in-law was a strange but brilliant man. He played the violin with the Houston Symphony as a child. He patented numerous inventions. He graduated from Rice University at such an early age that he had to defer matriculation to medical school at the University of Texas for two years. Before the age of twenty-six, he'd graduated first in his class at medical school; served as a doctor in the U.S. military; and been awarded a research fellowship at the National Institutes of Health, where he isolated a cold virus. His name was Leon Trotsky Atlas.

LEON'S PARENTS, MJ AND FANNIE ATLAS, fled Russian-controlled areas of Poland and Belarus where Cossack-led pogroms and repressive Tzarist policies threatened the lives and livelihoods of Eastern European Jews in the late nineteenth and early twentieth centuries. To them, Leon Trotsky, along with Lenin and

Stalin, was a hero. He was the man who had led the Red Army to victory against Tzarist forces in the October Revolution and forever changed the course of history.

But after World War II, as virulent anti-Communist sentiment spread throughout the United States, Leon's name became a serious liability. To put it into context, being named for Leon Trotsky during the Red Scare would have been something akin to being named Ulysses S. Grant in the South after the Civil War or Osama bin Laden in the U.S. after 9/11. Leon grew to hate his name—which brought him only trouble and hardship in the late 1940s and early 1950s—and spent most of his adult life trying to hide the fact that he'd been named for the famous Russian revolutionary.

But I was curious about Leon Trotsky and wanted to know more about the man who'd inadvertently played a role in the demise of my father-in-law's promising medical research career at the NIH. So, on a warm day in February 2010, after visiting Frida Kahlo's house in Mexico City, two friends and I walked over to see Casa Trotsky, the place where Leon Trotsky, known to his cadre of young male secretaries as the "Old Man," had once lived.

❋ ❋ ❋

COYOACÁN IS A TRANQUIL, LEAFY NEIGHBORHOOD in the southwest part of Mexico City, with wide boulevards and a large colorful market. But it is best known for being home to the Casa Azul. Tourists queue up to visit Frida Kahlo's house every day except Mondays, when it's closed, to catch an intimate look behind the tall Mediterranean-blue walls that fill the corner of Allende and Londres streets. A few blocks away, yet often overlooked, is the Museo Casa de León Trotsky.

My friend Patrice, who led tours of Mexico City for years, warned me not to bother. "It's incredibly ugly and not very interesting," she said.

I had to agree: Casa Trotsky is not beautiful like Frida's house is. But our visit proved interesting, mostly due to a quirky young Trotskyite—maybe the last in Mexico—who helped me better understand the man my father-in-law was named for.

I'D JUST PURCHASED A TICKET when a waifish young woman wearing a red Museo Leon Trotsky T-shirt and baggy khakis approached and asked me in Spanish if I would like a guided tour of the house and museum. Unlike most guides I've toured Mexican museums with, she had trouble making eye contact with me and her voice was barely audible.

"¿Cuánto cuesta?" I asked, wanting to know the price before we committed.

"It's free," she mumbled, staring at her white tennis shoes as if they were the most interesting thing in the world.

I consulted my friends, who agreed to do the free tour.

"My name is Alma," she said in English as we gathered. "I speak Russian, German, French, English, and Spanish. Which language would you prefer?"

"English!" the three of us chimed in unison.

I was impressed by the young woman's linguistic facility but a little worried about her health.

Poor Alma's skin made it look as if life for her were one massive allergen. Her face, neck, arms, and hands down to her fingertips were inflamed with eczema. Just looking at her made my skin itch. From her baggy clothing, slumped posture, and inability to look you in the eye, it seemed as if she might also have a problem with self-esteem.

But like a marionette whose strings have suddenly been pulled taut, Alma came to life as she led us through the muse-um's brightly lit halls, pointing out photos of Trotsky, his wife Natalia, and the many famous people surrounding them. She could name every person in the photographs and had fascinat-ing bits of gossip to share about each of their relationships to Trotsky. She recounted intimate stories about him as if he were a beloved uncle or her own grandfather: his falling out with Diego Rivera; his passion for collecting cactus; how he, himself, ministered to his beloved chickens and rabbits.

We also learned a fair bit of history from Alma that day. After Stalin sentenced him to death in absentia in 1929, Trotsky spent eleven years in exile, including two years in Norway. While the Norwegian Minister of Justice—working in collusion with Stalin—was preparing to ship him and Natalia to a remote island in the North Sea, word arrived that Mexican muralist Diego Rivera had convinced Mexican President Lázaro Cárdenas to grant the Trotskys asylum in Mexico. With all other possibilities exhausted, they arrived in Tampico in 1937 and settled in Coyoacán. First as guests of Diego and Frida at the Casa Azul, and later at their own homely enclave on Avenida Viena.

ALMA LED US OUT OF THE MUSEUM to the drab cluster of brick and stucco buildings that make up Casa Trotsky. According to her, the house and grounds had been preserved exactly as they appeared when the Trotskys lived there and this wasn't hard to believe. The colorless group of depressing-looking buildings had a narrow sliver of garden and was surrounded by a twelve-foot crudely cobbled stone wall. Empty chicken coops, rabbit hutches and patches of cactus, spiky dracaena and boxwood hedges provided the only respite from the house's austere façade, which looked more like a minimum-security prison than a home. Trotsky's grave marker—the garden's centerpiece—matched the house in humility: a simple granite monolith with his name engraved above a prominent hammer and sickle.

She told us Trotsky had spent the last years of his life relentlessly working—dictating letters, writing articles and books on the lives of Lenin and Stalin, publishing manifestos, and fighting to restore his standing on the world's political stage. His driving personality bordered on hypomania and he not only exhausted himself, but also the young men who served as his secretaries and bodyguards. Another manifestation of Trotsky's mania included grandiose plans to overthrow capitalism on a world scale—the Fourth International, as he referred to it.

"During the last weeks of his life, a delegation of Minnesota Socialists arrived in Coyoacán to present Lev (Trotsky's Russian nickname) with a plan to start a revolution in the United States," Alma said in a conspiratorial tone. It amused me to imagine Trotsky encouraging a band of sturdy Minnesotans to subvert the good men and women of Lake Wobegon.

When not working obsessively, Trotsky inclined toward depression. During his many years in exile, Stalin tortured, killed, or exiled most of his family and many of his closest comrades in the U.S.S.R.

"The terrible news arriving from Europe distressed Lev greatly," Alma said. His daughter Zinaida committed suicide in Berlin after her daughter and husband disappeared. His son Lyova was murdered in Paris by the G.P.U. (precursor to the K.G.B.), and his other daughter died of tuberculosis.

Trotsky himself was troubled with ill health; he had high blood pressure and a heart condition and was preoccupied with anxiety about his own death. In order to sleep at night, he took double doses of laudanum.

As WE TOURED THE TROTSKYS' BEDROOM and that of their grandson, Esteban Volkov (known to friends and family as Seva), the Old Man's despair felt almost palpable. Ironclad, prison-like doors opened on to dreary, olive-colored rooms where the walls were pocked with dozens of bullet holes from an assassination attempt led by painter David Alfaro Siqueiros in May 1940. Among the room's spartan furnishings were the narrow iron beds Trotsky and Seva hid under the night Siqueiros and his band of drunken Stalinists, dressed in stolen Mexican police uniforms—supposedly working in tandem with a traitorous security guard named Sheldon Harte—shot the place up with crude machine guns.

The adjoining room, Trotsky's study, was slightly cheerier. A map of Mexico covered the wall behind his desk, and along an adjacent wall, a large stained-glass window let in the bright afternoon light. His long wooden desk was surrounded by old-fashioned straight-backed chairs, an ancient Dictaphone, and bookcases packed with leather-bound books. In addition to being the room where Trotsky wrote many of his most famous letters and manifestos, this was the place where a man named Ramón Mercader, upon orders from Stalin, plunged an ice axe into the Old Man's brain on August 20, 1940. Twenty-four hours later, Leon Trotsky was dead. He was sixty years old.

THE LEADER OF THE BOLSHEVIKS never abandoned his commitment to revolution as the means to achieving worldwide socialism. In "Trotsky's Testament," written six months before his assassination, he said: "I shall die a proletarian revolutionist, a Marxist, a dialectic materialist, and, consequently, an irreconcilable atheist. My faith in the communist future of mankind is not less ardent, indeed it is firmer today, than it was in the days of my youth."

AS OUR TOUR WITH ALMA drew to a close, I couldn't help asking her about Trotsky's relationship to Frida Kahlo. According to Frida's biographer, Hayden Herrera, Trotsky was a known womanizer. In *Frida: A Biography of Frida Kahlo* Herrera claims the two of them had an affair. She also said that Frida was the one who ended it, being bored with el Viejo. But it was Natalia, angry and brokenhearted upon discovering it, who insisted they move out of the Casa Azul. When I asked Alma about it, she vigorously defended Trotsky.

"There is absolutely no evidence that Lev had an affair with Frida Kahlo. His grandson, Seva, is a friend of mine. He also disputes the affair!"

Being so firm in her conviction, I decided not to argue. I had no desire to offend her or Seva Volkov, who, according to

Alma, was now in his late eighties and lived only a few blocks from the museum.

In the last room on the tour—a dormitory-like quarters where Trotsky's secretaries and guards slept—I decided to share with Alma the thing my father-in-law had spent a lifetime trying to hide.

"My father-in-law was named after Leon Trotsky," I told her.

"Really?" Her watery eyes brightened.

"Yes, really. He was a medical doctor in the United States."

WHAT I DIDN'T TELL ALMA was how Leon's classmates at Rice University openly booed when his full name was read aloud at commencement. I also didn't tell her about the time the FBI showed up unexpectedly at the National Institutes of Health—where he and my mother-in-law worked—and interrogated them both about Leon's work and outside activities at the behest of the House Un-American Activities Committee. I didn't tell her that being named for a Bolshevik revolutionary hadn't helped his career and had likely contributed to the loss of his research fellowship at the NIH and a promised position at Baylor Medical School. All because his mother, who was also interrogated by the FBI, had been a member of the Communist Party USA in the 1930s and 1940s.

Not long before my visit to Casa Trotsky, my mother-in-law, Maxine, informed me that after her ex-husband lost his research fellowship at the NIH, they moved north to Boston where he did a fellowship in infectious diseases at Peter Bent Brigham Hospital. After the fellowship, his plan had been to return to Houston where he'd been promised a job at Baylor University's Medical School. But Baylor too withdrew their offer. For years my husband speculated that the FBI gave officials at Baylor the excuse they were looking for to rescind their job offer to his father. While impossible to prove, we do know that after receiving the news Leon fell into a severe depression that lasted a year, leaving my mother-in-law to figure out how to house and clothe and feed four children under the age of five. And I don't believe it was mere coincidence that Leon's breakdown occurred shortly after Julius and Ethel Rosenberg were executed.

But I didn't tell Alma any of this that day at Casa Trotsky.

"His name was Leon Trotsky Atlas," I said, wanting to pay tribute to the man and his name for one of the few people in the world who might actually appreciate it.

"Leon... Trotsky... Atlas," she repeated slowly. "That is *such* a beautiful name. I must go and tell Seva about this tonight!"

Oaxacan Mercy

FOR MORE THAN FIFTEEN YEARS my friend Muriel and I have traveled around Mexico visiting and interviewing the country's most respected artisans. However, the one place we'd never been together was Oaxaca. We decided that, come hell or high water, 2016 was the year we would finally go. After months of going back and forth, we settled on the first week of October. But by late September, I wasn't sure I'd be able to join my traveling companion after all.

My business partners and I were selling City People's Mercantile, the last of four retail stores we'd owned and operated in Seattle since 1979. Though a deal with the buyers had been in the works for months, the Small Business Administration was holding things up. More forms needed to be filled out. More supporting documents submitted. More personal guarantees granted. Each week that it dragged on, the atmosphere at the store grew increasingly tense. None of us knew when—or even if—the deal was going to close; and yet the Seattle couple who planned to buy the business insisted on spending time there. The employees felt as if they suddenly had two sets of bosses and were not particularly happy about it. Living in a state of limbo and confusion was tough on everyone: sales were floundering, attitudes tanking, employees quitting.

For me, it was becoming clear just how hard it was going to be to hand over a business I'd started at age twenty-six and managed for thirty-seven years to two people I barely knew. No matter how eager I'd been to sell six months before, I wasn't at all confident that my store and I were going to be able to get along without each other. Being the founder of City People's, a small chain of beloved urban general stores, had defined my entire adulthood. I loved my job as head buyer and merchandise manager and I loved the people I worked with.

IN THE CHAOTIC WEEKS following our public announcement of the sale, doubt and insecurity began to elbow out my normally confident self. Questions nagged at me: Who was I if I was no longer the owner of City People's? My stores had not only provided a decent living for my family, my sense of self was inextricably entwined with them. How would I fill my days without my job?

I'd read articles in the AARP magazine which claimed retirement was an opportunity to reinvent yourself, and to do all the things you hadn't had time for while working. I'd seen commercials with good-looking, silver-haired couples appearing to have the time of their lives on some beach or golf course. Being someone who doesn't golf and becomes bored after an hour at the beach, those articles and ads only brought up more uneasy questions. Was it really possible to reinvent oneself at my age? If so, what would the new me look like? I'd been writing for years, but it felt more like a hobby than a career, and a lonely one at that. One thing I'd learned about myself in my sixty-plus years on earth is that I need to feel connected and useful to be happy. Still, I wondered: even if I found people and things to fill my days, would I ever feel truly useful again?

I also felt guilty leaving my employees behind. In a small business the people you work with are like family. Many of our employees had been with us for ten, fifteen, and some of them, twenty years or more. I'd spent more waking hours with the employees, my business partners and sales reps than I had with my actual family over the last thirty-seven years. Our staff's happiness and job satisfaction had always been important to me. I felt like a mother hen abandoning her brood.

To make matters worse, the debauched 2016 presidential campaign was in full swing. And despite his bombastic, self-aggrandizing tweets and the hateful, racist, misogynist drivel he spewed at his rallies, Donald Trump was gaining in the polls. This only added to my despair. When October 1 rolled around and the buyers still didn't have a firm closing date, I announced to my partners that I was leaving for Oaxaca anyway. I flew to Mexico on October 4 with a plan to remain there until the election was over and the deal was done. A psychologist would have labeled it classic avoidance behavior.

❀ ❀ ❀

I FIRST TRAVELED TO OAXACA aboard the Oaxaqueño train from Mexico City with my college boyfriend and four friends from San Miguel. We were six happy hippies, aged sixteen to twenty-nine, in search of blissful beaches, cheap accommodations, and a panoply of psychedelic experiences. We found those things and much more in the place the Náhuatl called Huaxyacac, place of the *huaje* trees.

In the early 1970s, the bright white Oaxaca International Airport, with its shiny tile floors and friendly tourist information agents, didn't exist. If there was an airport in Oaxaca at the time, no one I knew could afford to fly there. It would be fifteen or twenty more years before regular folks began flying into Oaxaca. To get there in 1974 you had to travel southwest from Mexico City by bus, train, or car—if you had one. No matter how you chose to travel, it took hours.

My friends and I were only in the state of Oaxaca for ten days but my little-girl-from-Kansas outlook on life was forever transformed by the surrealistic adventures inherent in traveling on the cheap in Mexico in the 1960s and 1970s. I remember accidentally checking into a bordello where my boyfriend was solicited by an emaciated Mexican girl; a terrifying ten-hour second-class bus trip on a narrow unpaved road through the

Sierra Madre; a peyote trip in Zipolite that went from bad to worse. Being part of a group that was held at gunpoint and robbed by two Mexican federal police officers in a coconut grove at midnight and then drinking beer, the following night, with the same man who'd robbed us.

I'm forty-two years older now. I fly into Oaxaca's gleaming, light-filled airport, am fairly fluent in Spanish, and no *federale* would get the better of me today without at least a discussion. I no longer check into brothels to save money and gave up experimenting with hallucinogenic drugs years ago. Still, my latest trip to the Valley of Oaxaca turned out to be as full of surprises as my first. Some of them delightful, others quite disturbing.

The first surprise was discovering how cosmopolitan Oaxaca had become since I'd last visited in 1998 for the city's premier cultural festival, the Guelaguetza. Five-star restaurants, upscale cafés, art galleries, and chic boutiques abound. On our first day, Muriel and I lunched at Casa Oaxaca where *huitlacoche* (corn fungus), *chapulines* (grasshoppers), and *gusanos de maguey* (Maguey larvae) highlight the menu. Once considered disgusting by tourists and déclassé by wealthy Mexicans, native ingredients such as worms and insects, and flights of locally made Oaxacan mezcal are now celebrated by chefs at posh restaurants across Mexico.

THAT EVENING WE WANDERED by the Macedonio Alcalá Theater and got last-minute tickets to a concert by the Pasatoño Orquestra, a local group of ethnomusicologists dedicated to preserving and playing traditional Oaxacan-village orchestral music and their own style of *música Mixteca*. A curious mix of violins, clarinets, trumpets, and guitars, as well as indigenous instruments, were used to play tunes that ranged from jazzy danceable melodies to soporific ballads. Rubén Luengas Pérez, the group's leader, played the *Bajo quinto*, a deep-throated, five-stringed guitar made in only two villages in Oaxaca.

Afterwards we stopped in at a sidewalk café on Oaxaca's famous zócalo for a late supper. The lively square was crowded with locals and many of the women were dressed in traditional Oaxacan *huipiles* and *rebozos*. Watching them parade past our table in their colorful crimson, cerulean, plum, and magenta embroidered blouses and shawls made my favorite sport of people watching even more interesting. As is often true in Mexico, the intense colors and friendly people were a balm to my soul. Oaxaca's animated central plaza; delicious Oaxacan *comida*; lively Mixtecan music; its verdigris *cantera* stonework; and cornflower blue, russet, and sunny-yellow walls conspired to lift my spirits.

❀　❀　❀

THE PLAN FOR THE WEEK was to visit a number of artisans in the valley south of Oaxaca City. Our first stop was the village of Ocotlán de Morelos, to see an exhibition of paintings by Rodolfo Morales and visit the town's lively market. Teeming with people, produce, and *pan,* the market at Ocotlán is one of Mexico's finest. Piles of *bolillos* and rich Mexican choco-late; baskets full of crimson-colored *chapulines;* and white flour tortillas, the size of small *sombreros*, were being hawked by dark-skinned, stocky women in flowery *huipiles*. "*¿Que va a llevar?*" or "*¿Que gustaría güerita?*" they called out but when I politely asked in Spanish if I could take their photo, each one waved me off. Even with the ever-present reality of selfies and cell phone photography, Oaxacan women's attitudes had not changed in regard to having their photos taken—they're as resistant today as they were forty years ago.

JUST STEPS FROM THE MARKET we found the convent of Santo Domingo de Ocotlán, a lovely monastery-turned-museum that houses a major collection of Rodolfo Morales's paintings. In the pleasant, airy walkways surrounding an open courtyard, it was easy to imagine clusters of monks or nuns wandering about with silent supplications forming on their lips.

The paintings of the man they called El Señor de los Sueños are truly dreamlike and surrealistic. After Morales died of pancreatic cancer in 2000, an *L.A. Times* obituary writer called him "a guiding spirit of Oaxacan art and an heir to the artistic legacy of Rufino Tamayo." I found Morales's fanciful paintings more Chagall-like than reminiscent of Tamayo. Like much of Chagall's work, they were full of colorful figures—in particular, female figures—who float above the earth or are covered in flowers. When asked about the meaning of his work, the Gentleman of Dreams demurred, saying only that *"La nostalgia y la melancolía son muy importantes para mí."*

OUR SECOND STOP IN OCOTLÁN was the workshop of Josefina Aguilar, a prizewinning ceramic artist whose work Muriel and I had seen at *concursos* (juried competitions) in Pátzcuaro and Uruapan in Michoacán and at the National Ceramics Fair in Tlaquepaque. Muriel had visited the Taller Aguilar before, but had only a vague notion of where the workshop was located, so our driver, Octavio, stopped at a Pemex station to inquire. As often happens in Mexico, as soon as Muriel said, "Gas station attendants here never know where anything is, even if it's right under their noses," the gods contradicted her. Octavio jumped back in the car and took us directly there.

Josefina Aguilar first gained international recognition as a ceramic artist when Nelson Rockefeller began collecting her work in the early 1970s. Since then, she's become one of Mexico's most sought-after folk artists. Her popular *muñecas,* whimsical clay figures, often dressed like Frida Kahlo in traditional Tehuana dress and ranging from ten inches to three feet tall, fill the shelves at her workshop. They also can be found in the folk-art collections of museums all over the world, including the Museo de Arte Populare in Mexico City, the International

Folk Art Museum in Santa Fe, and the Rockefeller wing of the San Antonio Art Museum.

Still regal, despite her graying hair and deeply lined face, Señora Aguilar was seated at a small table in the *taller's* patio when we arrived. She stared straight ahead, making no gesture of welcome or greeting as we walked into the patio. Her laconic indifference to our arrival felt awkward; I wondered if visitors annoyed her or if something was wrong.

A younger woman approached us and explained: *"Mi madre es ciega,"* she said. Her mother was blind. Señora Aguilar had lost her eyesight two years earlier.

As I wandered about the studio admiring the señora's colorful clay figures, I wondered how a visual artist could continue working without her sight. And if she had fallen into depression because of it. Her daughter responded, as if she'd read my mind. "My mother can still 'feel' the clay and she works with it every day," she said. "It's the one thing that still brings her happiness."

HER WORDS DEEPLY AFFECTED ME and made me rethink a question I've pondered for a long time: Why is it that some people are resilient in the face of adversity while others fall apart? When faced with such a formidable obstacle—which we are bound to be at some point—what would we do? Collapse in self-pity? Or carry on as best we are able, as Josefina Aguilar?

When Muriel and I each bought a muñeca (clay doll), Señora Aguilar surprised us by graciously agreeing to a photograph.

        ❀   ❀   ❀

SOON AFTER WE ARRIVED IN OAXACA, Muriel, who is an opera buff, discovered that the Metropolitan Opera was live-streaming Wagner's *Tristan und Isolde* at the Macedonio Alcalá Theater on Saturday morning. Being an opera lightweight, I'd opt for Puccini over a Nazi sympathizer's heartbreaking opera about love and death any day. But after a delicious breakfast of a mango smoothie and banana pancakes at the Pan AM restaurant, I was actually looking forward to it. I remember feeling genuinely happy the morning we hurried down Oaxaca's sun-dappled streets towards the theater.

But, once there, sitting in the dark, half-empty nineteenth century baroque playhouse, watching an equally dark German opera about ill-fated lovers, felt like a strange thing to be doing on such a beautiful day in one of Mexico's most colorful cities. Midway through the opera, things turned even stranger and darker when my phone lit up with a text from my business partner Dianne. "Can you call me? Or check your email?"

IN A DIM HALLWAY outside the theater's restrooms, I reached Dianne. She had bad news. Our employee Seb had committed suicide. I sank to the floor. Seb was the third employee we'd lost to suicide in the past ten years.

"When?" I asked.

"They died last night," she said.

I was baffled. Why was she saying *they*? Had multiple people committed suicide?

"Did she commit suicide *with* someone?"

"No, they were alone," Dianne said.

"Why do you keep saying *'they*?"

"According to Seb's sister, it was their preferred gender pronoun. I didn't realize it, and I guess you didn't either, but Seb was transitioning."

I was stunned.

Few of their coworkers, or us, their bosses, knew much about Seb's personal life. I assumed they were a lesbian, as many of the women who work at City People's are, but I had no idea they were changing genders. Because they worked out in the garden center and I worked inside the store, we'd had little chance to interact. What I did know was that they reminded me of a Midwestern farmer. Sturdy, stoic, taciturn, hardworking. They wore John Deere caps, plaid shirts, and heavy-duty leather boots.

Their one nod to vanity was changing the color of their hair every week. One week it would be green, the next week, pink.

While we'd had little interaction, I distinctly remembered a conversation we had out in the nursery one day. I'd asked them how their job was going.

"Best place I've ever worked," they said. "I've never had a job where I felt as accepted as I do here." Then they added, "I really like the folks who work here, they're good people."

That brief conversation kept turning over in my head as I sat in the darkened hallway trying to digest the news. I wondered if our decision to sell the store had had anything to do with their suicide. Could one more major transition have pushed them over the edge?

I made my way back to my seat. But I didn't stay seated for long. I couldn't. When Isolde discovered that her lover Tristan had been killed and began slicing her arms with a knife, I retreated to my hotel room. Muriel went to lunch alone.

LATER THAT AFTERNOON, I pulled myself together and walked over to the Basílica de Nuestra Señora de la Soledad. A huge banner with the words MISERICORDIA EN OAXACA hung over the door of the seventeenth century church. Oaxacan Mercy. The centerpiece of the lavish basilica is its jewel-crowned icon of the Virgin of Solitude. La Soledad is believed to possess great healing powers; pilgrims come from all over Mexico to pray for miracles only she can perform. I lit a candle for Seb and asked the virgin to protect them as they transitioned into their next life. I prayed it would be a more merciful one.

Sitting alone in the basilica's lovely gold-encrusted sanctuary, I also made a decision: to return to Seattle as soon as possible. I knew where I needed to be and it wasn't Mexico. For the sake of my employees, my business partners, and the future of the business I needed to stop avoiding the inevitable changes coming my way and return to Seattle to help comfort the employees and make the transition to the new ownership as smooth as possible.

* * *

THE SOONEST I COULD GET A FLIGHT BACK to Seattle was Wednesday. Muriel left for San Miguel on Monday morning, so I spent those last two days in Oaxaca by myself, which was fine. I needed time alone. On Tuesday I wandered around the city and spent several peaceful hours in the Museum of Oaxaca at the Santa Domingo Church. I visited the Textile Museum and the San Pablo Cultural Center to see a retrospective on the life of Justina Oviedo Rangel, a renowned weaver from San Mateo del Mar on the Oaxacan coast. Señora Rangel's early life had been one of extreme poverty and deprivation, but her art—lovely, delicate cotton weavings of whimsical birds and animals and palm trees—transcended those hardships. Her long and productive creative life and the beauty of her weavings were an inspiration.

THE AFTERNOON WAS BRIGHT AND WARM. I sat on an iron bench in Oaxaca's zócalo for a long time, watching children chase soap bubbles around the square and thinking about how precious and fleeting—and also how challenging—this bodily incarnation can be. I thought of Justina Ovieda Rangel and Josefina Aguilar and Rodolfo Morales who, despite illness, blindness, and poverty, had all managed to stay productive and creative well into old age. I thought about Seb and how profoundly they must have suffered. I thought about my own past bouts with depression and my ongoing struggle with uncertainty, aging, and change. I thought about how life just keeps moving along, regardless of how we feel about it.

I also thought about Oaxaca's patron saint, the benevolent Virgen de la Soledad, and of the mercy and compassion she bestows on the pilgrims who visit her. I prayed she would help me navigate the impending tumult I was certain to face in the coming year.

* * *

MY PARTNERS, OUR EMPLOYEES, AND THE NEW OWNERS of City People's were all grateful for my return. On my first day back at work, the news of Seb's death was still fresh and feelings raw. We did our best to comfort each other and avoided trying to explain what is inexplicable. But the idea that our selling the store—a place where Seb felt safe and welcome—might have contributed to their despondency continued to haunt me.

I LEARNED FROM A CO-WORKER THAT, prior to their suicide, Seb had been planning an art show called "F~k My Tits" to raise funds for breast removal surgery. Seb worked at City People's to earn a living, but first and foremost, they were an artist, a nature-lover, and a shaman. After news of their death got out, their friends decided to host the art show anyway, as a celebration of their life. On a dismal, rainy October night, my two business partners and I drove over to the Muse Gallery in West Seattle.

In stark contrast to the unexpectedly festive atmosphere inside the brightly lit room, Seb's paintings were flooded with dark, disturbing imagery. Women's sliced up bodies with worms or violets sprouting from their nakedness. Bodies with plants or flowers in lieu of heads and limbs. Asparagus, ivy, and dogwood flowers sprouting from children's frowning faces. Most disturbing was a self-portrait: a crouched and naked Seb, wearing a devastated expression as strange flowers and green ribbons flowed from their rent heart. The parallels between their art and the paintings of Mexico's most celebrated female artist were irrefutable. Like Frida's, Seb's paintings were a visual testimony to the depth of personal despair. And one thing was clear to my partners and me—their downward trajectory had been set in motion long before they ever came to work at City People's.

January 2018

I'VE RETURNED TO OAXACA and am seated once again on a pew in the Basílica de la Soledad. The church's patron saint, with her gilded mantle and drop-pearl crown, appears as splendid and radiant as I remembered and her calm countenance radiates warmth like a loving embrace. Among the pilgrims gathered at her feet today are an ancient *abuelita* in a wheelchair; a lively, chatty three-year-old attached to an oxygen tank by a plastic tube in his nose; and a young couple cradling a swaddled newborn in their arms.

Whispered prayers and supplications float on the air as I sit alone in the next to last pew. Unlike the others, I'm not here today to pray to or solicit the virgin's help. I'm here to express my gratitude for the blessings she's bestowed upon me since I last visited her. Despite my nagging doubts, I managed to navigate the multiple major transitions of the past year. It wasn't easy. But there was enough grace and more equanimity than I would have thought possible.

RETIREMENT, AS IT TURNS OUT, SUITS ME. I am constantly recommending it, especially to friends who are exhausted and unhappy with their jobs, but can't quite make the leap. I find myself as busy, or busier than ever, with projects I find fulfilling and worthwhile. I edited and published a new bilingual anthology for the San Miguel Literary Sala that we'll launch the end of this month and I'll be teaching at their writers' conference in February. And with a second book in the works, I guess writing actually is more than just a hobby.

City People's seems to be doing as well without me as I am without it. I still think about Seb and miss my co-workers, but I can't say I miss my job. My store-identified ego-self has moved on.

Except for the presidency of Donald Trump, life is good. Each day I try to temper the chaos that that train wreck of a man creates every day by being kinder to the people around me and to myself. Sometimes that means tuning out the frenzied news cycles and turning inward for a while. And that's okay. We are all pilgrims in this unpredictable and worrisome world who need not only the merciful love of the virgin-mother, but also to be wellsprings of mercy and compassion for ourselves as well as for others.

Chiapan Journal

I LIKE TO think of myself as a conscientious traveler. When I travel—in Mexico or in any foreign country—I try to learn at least a little of the language and something about the customs and cultural norms. I adjust my behavior accordingly, even if it means changing my way of doing things and rethinking my expectations. This is especially necessary when I travel to parts of Mexico where there are large indigenous populations. For example, the state of Chiapas.

El estado libre y soberano de Chiapas—the Free and Sovereign State of Chiapas—with its remote and mountainous landscape is home to masked rebels and some of the best coffee in North America. Rainforests, cloud forests, spectacular waterfalls; quetzals, horned iguanas, howler monkeys, and giant sloths can be found there. Palenque, one of the world's most important archeological sites, is also in Chiapas.

Mexico's southernmost state, which shares a border with Guatemala, is also the country's most diverse. There are thirteen different ethnic sub-groups in Chiapas and each speak their own particular Mayan dialect. The Tzotziles and Tseltales are the largest; the two make up about 70% of the indigenous population in and around San Cristóbal de las Casas, the state's most popular tourist destination.

Cultural norms and practices among Mexico's indigenous populations can be far more difficult for a gringa like me to understand than, say, the modernized Spanish-speaking populations of San Miguel de Allende or Mexico City. Despite how hard I try to be culturally sensitive, in March of 2019, when I traveled to Bachejón—a Tseltal town two hours northeast of San Cristóbal—as a guest of a Seattle NGO working in the area, I made a cultural faux-pas I soon came to regret. Figuring out how to atone for my mistake was a complicated calculation.

OUR SMALL CLUSTER OF DONOR-GUESTS arrived at the Misión de Bachajón after dark and a young priest named Jesús welcomed us. He spoke English well and reminded me of my friend Chip, physically and personality-wise. Like Chip, who was once a seminarian himself, Jesús laughed a lot and enjoyed telling humorous stories.

After settling into my monastic quarters, I headed to the dining room with the rest of our group for a self-serve dinner with the mission's priests-in-training. I was surprised at how hip the young Jesuits seemed. Long-haired and bearded, and dressed in loose fitting yoga pants or blue jeans, T-shirts and Birkenstocks, the seminarians looked like a bunch of guys my thirty-year-old son might hang out with.

The next day, after breakfast at the mission, we all walked over to a covered basketball court in the center of town where the concrete bleachers were quickly filling with locals. Soon a parade of men and boys dressed in vests made of Spanish moss and *sombreros de paja* filed up a side street and onto the court. Many of them carried mummified howler monkeys which I've since learned represent animal spirits. When I reached for my cellphone to snap a pic, Jeannie, the director of the NGO, waved me off. "It's probably not a good idea to take photos here."

BEING AVERSE TO CLUSTERING with other gringos at indigenous fiestas and hankering to sneak a few photos of the strange ritual, I moved away from our group. On the far side of the basketball court, I mingled with the locals and struck up a conversation with a fish biologist named José Manuel. He told me he was working in the Yucatán, but that his job would be ending soon. He was intrigued to hear that my son is also a fish biologist. In Vancouver, Canada. He asked if maybe Will could get him a job in Canada.

Three little girls—maybe seven or eight years old and dressed in bright red and yellow dresses—began running in circles around the basketball court alongside a group of men that José Manuel told me were the capitanes. Like the girls, the capitanes were dressed in red and yellow uniforms and fancy hats with foot-long, multi-colored ribbons streaming behind. José Manuel introduced me to his uncle who was one of the capitanes. I questioned him about the meaning of the race.

"If you want to understand the significance of the race," he said, "You'll have to talk with the principales after the event is over." I asked if it was okay to take photos and he said it was fine. (Though I have to admit here that, in addition to Jeannie, another man had warned me not to take photos). I assumed the Capitán, so nobly dressed in his red and yellow uniform, had more say so than either Jeannie or the man who said no. I ignored the warnings and keep snapping away.

AFTERWARDS, AS OUR GROUP of Seattleites walked through town to a nearby neighborhood, I couldn't help feeling conspicuous. We were, after all, the only foreigners in town. My American clothing alone made me stand out because every woman in Bachajón is dressed in traditional Tseltal fashion; crisp white blouses with scooped necklines adorned with wide strips of cross stitch (a technique introduced to the area by nuns in the 1930s) and lace yokes; and dark-blue or black wraparound skirts with shiny silver threads running through them. The Tseltal women of the neighborhood greeted Jeannie warmly and offered us pozol, a thick corn-and-cacao-based drink.

At the top of a hill, the celebration's prinicipales (bosses, more of less) were gathered around a table under a make-shift palapa. Jeannie explained to the group that the men were collecting donations on behalf of the community. The Capitán I'd met at the basketball court recognized me and waved me over.

After a few minutes of friendly small talk, he suggested I make a donation as payment for the photographs I'd taken.

"What kind of donation?" I asked.

"Una bolsa de arroz y una de frijol," he said. More than happy to provide a bag of rice and a bag of beans, I asked him where I might buy them. Just then, Jeannie and Miguel, one of the priests-in-training, spotted me chatting with the man and intervened when they learned that we were negotiating a donation. They didn't think it was a good idea for me to donate anything to the principales.

"It might set up the expectation that we'll continue to tithe them in the future," Jeannie said. I saw her point, but argued that providing a few bags of rice and beans didn't seem like much. But she and Miguel were insistent and after going back and forth for a few minutes, I gave in. I was, after all, there as a guest of the NGO. Plus, I'd been asked not to take photographs and I'd done it anyway. I turned back to the Capitán.

"I'm sorry, but I cannot give the principales rice and beans."

"But señora, you must!" he said. "Many photographers come here and take photos and sell them for a lot of money. One man got three-hundred-dollars for a photo and our community got nothing. It is only fair that you give something in return."

I agreed with him—it wasn't fair—but I felt hog-tied.

"I'll erase all of the photos and I promise not to write about the Tzeltal ritual for a newspaper," I said, pulling out my phone. As I began erasing the photos in front of him, the man's face sank.

"I don't understand," he said. I felt badly about the negative turn the day has taken. There seemed to be nothing I could do that would make everyone happy. I'd screwed up.

AT LUNCH THAT DAY, Padre Pepe, a charming blue-eyed priest who's spent much of his life working to improve the lives of the

Tseltales in and around Bachajón, explained the significance of the race we'd watched that morning. The ritual, he said, was meant to drive away evil spirits during la Cuaresma (Lent).

After lunch, still feeling contrite about the morning's misstep, I cornered the good padre in the kitchen.

"Father, I have something to confess."

I then told him the whole story: how I'd taken photographs even though I'd been told not to; how I'd been asked for a dona-tion but then was told it wasn't a good idea; how my actions had resulted in disappointment and misunderstanding. It felt good to get it off my chest. But I also told the good padre that I still wanted to do something for the community and asked what would be appropriate.

"It would be fine for you to buy sugar, rice, salt or oil and give it to the community," Father Pepe said. "But don't give them beans, they grow those themselves."

I went to the mission church that evening where Father Pepe delivered mass in both Spanish and Tseltal. When he invited those of us from Seattle to stand up at the altar with him, I felt conspicuous. For the first time in ten years, I took communion.

THE NEXT MORNING, I awoke feeling sick and feverish. When the group left for Toniná, a nearby archaeological site, I stayed behind. Despite feeling dreadful, I showered and got dressed and then managed to find my way back to the neighborhood where the festival took place. At a local tienda I bought six bags of rice, two bags of salt and two of sugar and paid two twelve-year-old girls ten pesos each to deliver it all to the prin-cipales. I suspected tongues might have been wagging in the neighborhood that afternoon, but the next morning I awoke with a clear conscience and feeling well enough to travel on to San Cristóbal de las Casas.

PART III ❀ DESVIACIONES

Photo of a poster on a wall in Oaxaca

Rationalism and doctrinarism are the disease of our time; they pretend to have all the answers. But a great deal will yet be discovered which our present limited view would have ruled out as impossible.
— C.G. Jung (1961)

Strange Days

DAY 1

Lightning strikes off the left wing of the Embraer jet I am flying in; the small plane shudders and drops fifty feet.

The jet's forty-some passengers and I gaze warily around, checking each other's reactions. Dallas is an hour behind us, Del Bajío International Airport an hour ahead and each of us aboard this American Airlines flight is wondering if we're going to make it. The Mexicans sitting next to me—a blue-jeaned rancher in a plaid shirt and white cowboy hat and a black-shawled, gray-haired grandmother—silently move their lips in prayer and cross themselves. I offer my own whispered prayers to the Virgin of Guadalupe, beseeching her to make sure the jet and its passengers arrive safely. We do.

The only casualty ends up being my computer, which I was working on when the pilot ordered us to stow all electronics and make sure our seat belts were fastened. When we finally pass through the storm and things calm down, I pull my laptop out again and try turning it on. The screen is blank.

THUNDERSTORMS PERSIST during the hour-and-a-half shuttle ride from the airport to San Miguel. July and August are "monsoon" season in Central Mexico, but heavy rains have continued through the month of September this year. At the turn off for Juventino Rosas, rain pummels the car and the already waterlogged landscape. Just outside San Miguel, cornfields are a foot under water and cattle moored like small boats in the sodden fields. Even San Miguel's train tracks—where San Miguel gossip says Neal Cassady died of a Seconal overdose in 1968—are inundated.

"In his movie on global warming Al Gore said Central Mexico would be a tropical landscape instead of desert some-day," announces the only other passenger in the car. She's an American from upstate New York who can't remember the documentary's name ("An Inconvenient Truth"), but this one piece of information has stuck in her head. I try to imagine the arid chaparral I've grown to love—a mix of mesquite and huizache, agave, nopal, sagebrush and echeveria—evolving into tropical rainforest, but it's too much of a stretch. Even with all this rain I can't muster a vision of Guanajuato's arid hills covered in palm trees, bromeliads, and thick tropical undergrowth. But I wonder, as I think many of us do: Does the excessive amount of rainfall we're experiencing indicate a major shift in the overall climate? Or is it merely a normal fluctuation? I'm not a climate change denier; still, it's hard to know what to think.

DAY 2

A strange, but nice thing happens
when I greet my neighbor Gracia.

I'm usually the one who initiates a hug, but for the first time in our thirteen-year friendship, Gracia throws her arms around me when I trot over to her store to tell her I'm back. She has a lot on her mind it turns out, and later in the day she shows up on my doorstep with two bowls of soup, made of broth, vegetables, and tiny meatballs that we eat while waiting for the computer repairman to arrive. She confides to me that her daughter is pregnant again. This baby will be Lupe's third and she's feeling a bit concerned. Lupe's had problems with the pregnancy and has been hospitalized twice with breakthrough bleeding.

"María Juana told Lupe that it's in God's hands and she shouldn't worry," Gracia says.

I tell my friend that God can only do so much, that sometimes we need to take responsibility. According to Gracia, no one is terribly happy about the pregnancy except Lupe's husband Juan. After two girls, he's counting on this one being a boy.

("¡Un *varón!*" my Spanish teacher, Griselda, says, shaking her head when we meet at San Miguel's Starbucks for a lesson the next day. There's a hint of disgust in her voice as she says: "Mexican men are fixated on having boys.")

In addition to Lupe's troubles, Gracia tells me she is worried about her son Marcos and his girlfriend, Verónica. They've split up and Verónica is now living at her mother's house with their three-year-old, Angel Daniel. Gracia worries about the effect his parent's split might have on her grandson.

THE COMPUTER REPAIRMAN shows up two hours late and runs all kinds of diagnostic tests. He eventually discovers the problem: the battery was jolted loose by the plane's sudden drop. He pulls it out, puts it back in, and my computer hums to life. I, on the other hand, am not so lucky.

DAY 3

I faint during meditation at Life Path Center
for the Healing Arts and am pronounced dead.

Feeling light-headed and slightly sick to my stomach, I put my head between my knees halfway through our forty-five-minute meditation session. When the chime rings, announcing the end of meditation, I sit up too quickly and the room spins wildly. Suddenly everything goes black. Within minutes my sangha friends have lowered me to the floor and a South African man named Athol is pressing his thumb into a vein in my wrist.

ANYONE WHO HAS FAINTED can attest that, although you are out cold, you can often still hear what people are saying. I once passed out with the bridesmaid's dress I was to wear in my oldest sister's wedding pinned on me with straight pins. I can still hear my mother shouting at the poor dressmaker: "Get the dress off of her! Get the dress off of her!" though it's never been clear whether it was me or the dress she was trying to save.

On the floor at Life Path, I can hear the alarm in Athol's voice as he tells the others in proper-sounding South African English: "I can't get a pulse! I can't get a pulse!" And then: "I think we've lost her!" In my fuzzy, semi-conscious state, I wonder: *Can you be dead and still hear people's voices?*

Someone runs over to the office to call La Cruz Roja's emergency response team. By the time the Red Cross team arrives ten minutes later, I'm awake but still on the floor, with Athol by my side. He's switched from taking my pulse to adjusting my chakras. As he busily hovers above me, I wonder if he's feeling sheepish about announcing I was code blue or if clearing chakras is a specialty of his.

The Red Cross team takes my blood pressure, checks my heart rate, and suggests I get something to eat and drink. They assure me I will be fine.

BREAKING NEWS LATER THE SAME DAY: Three busloads of students from a teacher's college in the state of Guerrero have gone missing. They will not be fine.

DAY 4

*Héctor Beltrán Leyva, a major Mexican drug lord,
is captured by federal agents at
Mario's Seafood Restaurant in San Miguel.*

One of four brothers who head Guerrero's notorious ABL cartel, Beltrán Leyva was a highly valued target for the Mexican government. A five-million-dollar reward had been offered for information leading to the arrest of the brothers, who are wanted for trafficking cocaine, heroin, marijuana, and metham-phetamines to Europe and the U.S. and for countless murders and kidnappings. Torture, human smuggling, money launder-ing, extortion, and gunrunning are mere sidelines for Héctor and his brothers.

NOT A SINGLE SHOT IS FIRED, and no resistance encountered as federal agents, backed up by a team of Navy Seal-like Mexican Marines, swarm a hole-in-the-wall seafood restaurant on Stirling Dickinson street in San Miguel's San Antonio neigh-borhood. It is a weeknight in early October and few others are there when soldiers storm the place and arrest Beltrán Leyva and his dinner partner, a Mexican businessman who is well-known in San Miguel circles. Expat friends are stunned—foreigners here like to think we're "safe" from the cartel troubles that plague border states and port cities in Mexico. Many downplay the news, as much to convince themselves they're not in any real danger as to keep friends and family in the States from becoming alarmed. Nevertheless, English lan-guage newspapers in San Miguel are sold out before noon the following day.

I BUY A COPY OF LA JORNADA and read about the arrest in Spanish but it's another headline in the paper that really captures my attention: "Auto-Defensa Ciudadana" (Citizen Self-Defense). The article is about mothers who are taking up arms in the state of Michoacán where cartel and gang violence have exploded in recent years. Accompanying the article is a photo of María de la Luz Sandoval standing in front of a Jeep Cherokee, cradling an AK-47. "Why shouldn't a mother defend her children?" reads the caption. Note in my journal that day: "Too much action in Mexico, even for me."

DAY 5

*It's four a.m. and the jardín, San Miguel's central plaza,
looks and sounds like the Battle of the Alamo.*

Exhausted from being kept up by my neighbor Julio who
was blasting egregiously bad 1970s and 1980s rock music from
his rooftop until dawn this morning, I watch the celebration of
La Alborada (which means "dawn") from my bedroom window
instead of walking down to the jardín at four a.m. to join in
the celebration.

SAN MIGUEL ARCÁNGEL, patron saint of San Miguel, is the
defender of the faithful. Every year, on or around September
29, a great battle ensues in the jardín between Saint Michael
and Lucifer, who persists in his annual revolt against God and
the powers of good in the world.

A man dressed as San Miguel brandishes his sword to drive
the devil out of town. Flares and rockets blast a papier-mâché
Lucifer. Fireworks bombard the tree-lined plaza, bursting above
the heads of spectators who have gathered before dawn to
watch the annual battle between good and evil. Even from my
bedroom perch high above the city, the exploding fireworks
pummel my eardrums and plumes of smoke fog the early morning
sky. The drama continues for over an hour and this is just the
beginning. We will spend the weekend celebrating San Miguel's
victory over the forces of evil with parades, fiestas, more fireworks, music, dancing, and indigenous costumes galore.

DAY 6

*The New York Times runs this gut-punch of a headline:
"43 Missing Students, A Mass Grave and a Suspect:
Mexico's Police."*

A mass grave containing 28 badly burned and dismembered
bodies was found outside the city of Iguala, Guerrero, the same

city where 43 young men from a local teacher's college disappeared the night of September 26. According to witnesses, police
officers first opened fire on busloads of students from a teacher's
college in Ayotzinapa, Guerrero, and then loaded the students
into police vehicles. All as a federal police officer watched. There
are also reports that a local drug cartel was involved.

WHY THE POLICE WOULD ATTACK unarmed nineteen- to twenty-
three-year-old students is beyond my comprehension. I am not
surprised, however, that the drug gang known as los Guerreros
Unidos has also been implicated. Local, and sometimes federal,
police forces and even state and local governments are infiltrated
by members of drug cartels in Mexico. This is no secret, even
to an ignorant *gringa* like me. But why would they attack,
dismember, and burn the bodies of twenty-year-old students?
I feel sick to my stomach and begin to weep, thinking of those
young men and their families.

DAY 7

I end up in San Miguel's Tech 100 Hospital.

I awake at one o'clock in the morning, but when I get out of
bed to go to the bathroom the room starts spinning madly. No
position except lying down again helps and even that doesn't
help much. I crawl to the bathroom and back to bed and lie
awake all night imagining the worst. In the morning I phone
Gracia, and she takes me in a taxi to see Dr. Gordillo on Hidalgo
street. The doctor asks a few questions, then sends me to the
emergency room at the Hospital de la Fe (now called the Tech
100) with a note asking them to admit me at once. There's
only one other patient there when we arrive; still, Gracia and
I wait for what seems like an interminably long time before I
am checked in. When check-in is completed, a young female
technician takes me into a small room and efficiently draws eight
vials of blood—by mistake. Turns out they only needed two.

"I need fluid to go in, not out!" I whine at the young woman in Spanish when she notes the mistake.

"I just do as I'm told," she says, which I know is true. Following orders is of paramount importance in Mexico. When a woman from the hospital's administration office comes in the room and asks for a deposit of seventy-five hundred pesos, it's Gracia's turn to lose it.

"¡*Te están robando!*" she says after the robber-woman steps out to run my credit card. "I was sick last month and had to go to the doctor," Gracia continues, mimicking vomiting. "He gave me medicine that made me feel better in only a few days. And for only thirty pesos!"

I try to explain that my health insurance in the U.S. will likely cover it and that I'm not going anywhere. She looks at me as if I've sprouted antennae. It's all alien to her: health insurance, credit cards, expensive private hospitals. After they put me in a private room and she realizes she will not be able to save me from the economic disaster I've embarked on, she gives up and hails a cab for home.

"When you're ready to get out of this place, call me," she says as she walks out the door. "I'll send Martín over to pick you up."

A SWEET NURSE, with creamy brown skin and teeth so white and perfect she could be a Cover Girl, spends the afternoon pumping me full of intravenous fluids. She also gives me an Ambien tablet to knock me out for the night. As the drug begins to work its magic (and my boundaries become blurred), I tell her she is the prettiest nurse in all of Mexico and ask what her name is. "Beatriz," she says. "Bay-ah-treez," I say, repeating her name slowly and enjoying the melodious sound of it on my tongue. Like Dante with his beloved Beatrice, I am spellbound. I say her name again and then fall into a deep sleep—for the first time in six days—with the face of the lovely Beatriz filling my head.

DAY 8

The mayor of Iguala and his wife go AWOL.

Four days after the 43 students disappear from the streets of Iguala, the town's mayor, José Luis Abarca, requests a leave of absence. Then he and his wife, María de los Ángeles Piñeda—who has family ties to the ABL cartel—disappear. A month later they will be apprehended in a run-down house in the Iztapalapa neighborhood of Mexico City but they will never be charged with any crime related to the 43 missing students, even though official documents later show that Abarca ordered the Iguala police "to teach them [the students] a lesson."

THE SAME DAY the mayor and his wife disappear, an independent search party made up of parents and members of an unarmed community police force fans out across an area called Pueblo Viejo in trucks and SUVs. Until a cartel boss sends a text message to the search party telling them that they need to back off or he will "fuck them up."

DAY 9

My husband flies to Mexico to rescue me.

After being released from the hospital, the perplexing vertigo persists. It appears to have nothing to do with being dehydrated, but Dr. Gordilla has no better diagnosis to offer. I Google "dizziness" to see what it might indicate and discover a range of possibilities. On the benign side: low blood pressure or low blood sugar, anemia, magnesium deficiency. More insidious causes: meningitis, abnormal heart activity, stroke, or brain tumor. Day after day, the dizziness, light-headedness, nausea, blurred vision, and unsteadiness continue to plague me. Rolling over in bed is like navigating eight-foot swells in a rowing punt; moving from a prone position to standing gives me the dry heaves. My husband, Paul, asks a friend to keep our two dogs and flies down to Mexico.

WE CALL THE MAN I jokingly refer to as Dr. Guapo, a handsome Mexican doctor who makes house calls and is popular with expat women in San Miguel. He's grayer than when I last saw him fifteen years ago for a terrible bout of *turista*, but still strikingly good-looking. He looks in my ears with an otoscope and immediately diagnoses the problem as an ear infection.

"Never put anything smaller than your elbow in your ear," he tells me. I assure him I haven't, but he ignores my response. "That was the advice of my adviser in medical school and it's good advice," he says cheerfully.

Paul and I enjoy our hour-long conversation with Dr. Guapo. We talk about San Miguel politics, the Affordable Care Act debacle, and the disturbing disappearance of the students in Guerrero—about which he offers a cynical shrug and says, "Welcome to Mexico!"

I pay the handsome doctor US$100 for his services, but within twenty-four hours of his visit it's clear he too has misdiagnosed the problem. Despite taking the antibiotics he gave me for my supposed ear infection, the room continues to spin.

DAY 10

The Governor of Guerrero resigns.

On October 11, the governor of the state of Guerrero, Ángel Aguirre, announces that forensic tests show that none of the remains of the 28 bodies found in Cocula belong to the 43 missing students. Protesters take to the streets in Iguala calling for his resignation. The remains of only two of the students will ever be positively identified, though Peña Nieto's government will insist on perpetuating the lie that the students were killed by members of Guerreros Unidos and burned in Cocula. They blame the lack of rule and governability of Guerrero on Aguirre but he is only a small cog in a much larger wheel of corruption.

A WEEK LATER

I fly back to Seattle with Paul.

The daily discoveries of what happened in Iguala shock and disturb me. The outpouring of anger and continuous street protests remind me of the Days of Rage, anti-war demonstrations in Chicago, 1969. But this is not the reason I leave Mexico; I leave because the spinning won't stop.

BACK IN SEATTLE, it will take three more months and two doctors at Group Health to definitively diagnose my problem as Benign Paroxysmal Positional Vertigo (BPPV)—likely caused by the whiplash I suffered when I fainted and my head snapped backwards. Once diagnosed, it is easily corrected with an Epley maneuver, a simple manipulation of the head, by a skilled physical therapist. However, I continue to be plagued by recurring neck pain, dizzy spells, and a light-headedness that never goes away. It impinges on my life in a number of ways: I can't do yoga or other exercise routines that require being upside down, I sleep poorly and seem to be more anxious than normal. Still, I am grateful. The diagnosis could have been far worse.

A MONTH LATER

"¡Vivos se los llevaron; vivos los queremos!"
becomes a rallying cry at protests across Mexico.

When parents of the missing students refuse to be cowed and demand answers from the Mexican government, they are invited to meet with President Enrique Peña Nieto. He and a slew of other bureaucrats—every one of them dressed like Peña Nieto clones in their signature gray suits with white-collared shirts and no neckties—meet with the parents at Los Pinos, the Mexican presidential palace.

Peña Nieto tries to brush the parents off with cliched answers and lame promises, but they resist; they refuse to leave until he signs a document agreeing to their demands—to search for the students alive, initiate an independent investigation, and hire the highly regarded Argentine Forensic Anthropology Team.

"¡Vivos se los llevaron; vivos los queremos!" ("They were taken alive; we want them back alive!") the parents chant at Peña Nieto as he exits the room.

FIVE MONTHS LATER

Lupe's third child is born.

THE FOLLOWING MARCH, Lupe's third baby arrives safely. Another girl. If Juan is disappointed, he doesn't show it. Samantha is pretty, chubby-cheeked, and healthy, and we all adore her. We also hope she's the last.

EIGHTEEN MONTHS LATER

While on a trip to Denmark, Peña Nieto announces the dissolution of the Inter-American Human Rights Commission.

In Guerrero, in Mexico City, in front of Mexican embassies and consulates across the globe, hundreds of thousands of protesters decry the kidnapping of the 43 young men from Ayotzinapa. Still, despite months of strikes, protests, and riots in Mexico City and in the state of Guerrero; despite vigils, pleas, and continuous pressure from family members; despite extensive media coverage and an outraged public; despite a global Internet campaign and the outrage expressed by the international panel of experts appointed to investigate the crimes, justice has not been served in the case of the 43 missing students.

The penultimate irony in all of this is that the students had commandeered the buses to transport them from Iguala to Mexico City so they could participate in an annual gathering to honor the students who died at the worst student massacre in Mexican history: the Tlatelolco Massacre. Official estimates say that on October 2, 1968, three to four hundred students and civilians were killed by military police at the Plaza de las Tres Culturas in Tlatelolco. Most Mexicans believe the number was three or four times that.

LESS THAN A YEAR AFTER being appointed by the International Human Rights Commission, the team charged with investigating the murders is forced to resign after being stonewalled and lied to by Mexican president Enrique Peña Nieto, his attorney general, and others in his government. The commissioners testified, based on evidence provided by the Argentine Forensics Team, that: "The government's claim that the students were killed and buried in a garbage dump by members of the Guerreros Unidos is scientifically impossible." They accused the government of torturing people for confessions, of not allowing them to interview officials from the 27th Battalion of Iguala who were directly tied to the case, and of turning a blind eye to the activities of drug lords who control large swathes of Guerrero. Questions about the missing students remain unanswered and protests continue to this day.

EVEN IF YOU DON'T SUFFER VERTIGO, the level of corruption and violence perpetrated against the Mexican people by their own government and the cartels would make your head spin. Half of state and local governments in the country are believed to be infiltrated by drug cartels or people affiliated with them; more than 106,000 people have died as a result of drug violence since Felipe Calderon declared war on the drug cartels in 2006; since 2016, 92 journalists have been murdered in Mexico for reporting on the drug cartels or government officials suspected of being affiliated with them; 22,000 people are currently missing in Mexico where 94 percent of crimes go uninvestigated. Meanwhile, the Mexican drug cartels' biggest market, the U.S., has failed to stem the demand for illegal drugs. Initiated by the Reagans, the War on Drugs has been an unmitigated disaster: overdose deaths have more than quadrupled in the last twenty years.

FIVE YEARS LATER

The parents of the missing students refuse to give up.

Many of the parents of the 43 missing students from Ayotzinapa still believe their sons are alive and that the Mexican government knows where they are. To this day they continue to protest, hold vigils and rallies, and to haunt government offices in search of the truth about what happened to their sons. A red and yellow banner with images of the forty-three missing students hanging in the courtyard of the teacher's college confirms their determination in giant letters: "SON, I WILL LOOK FOR YOU UNTIL I FIND YOU."

WHEN PEOPLE RISE UP and push back against violence and injustice in their communities, as these people have been doing for nearly five years, it gives me hope. Part of me even admires María de la Luz Sandoval, the gun-toting, ass-kicking bolt of lightning from Michoacán, with her "don't fuck with my children" message for the drug lords. But there's another, more insistent part of me, that believes more violence is not the answer. Still, how do people answer such violence and lies from their government?

SIX MONTHS AFTER THE STUDENTS DISAPPEARED, an enormous, fire-engine red +43 sculpture was erected at the corner of the Paseo de la Reforma and Avenida Juárez—a street that runs directly to the Zócalo, Mexico City's historic seat of power. Traveling down the Reforma in the back of a cab recently,

I spotted the bright red +43 and was reminded of lines from "Explico Algunas Cosas," a poem Pablo Neruda wrote after Franco's fascists murdered his friend, the poet Federico García Lorca, in 1936.

> *bandidos con frailes negros bendiciendo*
> *venían por el cielo a matar niños,*
> *y por las calles la sangre de los niños*
> *corría simplemente, como sangre de niños.*

> bandits with black friars spattering blessings
> came through the sky to kill children
> and through the streets the blood of children
> ran simply, like blood of children.

THE SCULPTURE, WITH ITS PROMINENT LOCATION, is a testament to Mexico's *desaparecidos* and an acknowledgement that the number 43 will never again be just a number to Mexicans. Like the date 9/11 is for Americans, it has become a cultural touchstone, one laden with implication. It carries the same oppressive weight the name Tlatelolco has carried since 1968 and is an unambiguous reminder that the struggle for a just and moral Mexico has yet to be won.

Submitting to El Chapo

WHILE PERUSING DUOTROPE'S Weekly Wire for places to submit my articles and essays about life in Mexico, I spotted a new literary journal called the *El Chapo Review*. Sounded Mexican all right—*el chapo* is a popular Spanish nickname which means "shorty." When I read that the new review was soliciting submissions for their first nonfiction essay contest and offering cash prizes, I took note.

It didn't occur to me that it had anything to do with the *real* El Chapo, Mexico's most notorious drug lord. I assumed it was a spoof made up by people who wanted to capitalize on his name or his recent interview with actor-turned-journalist Sean Penn. However, after checking out the *El Chapo Review's* inimitable website, and receiving several subsequent emails from them—including two rejections—I began to believe the *El Chapo Review* might actually be real and that somewhere in a high security prison cell in Mexico, Joaquín Archivaldo Guzmán Loera—head of the Sinaloa Cartel and one of the world's most wanted men—might actually have read my essay "Dreaming of Paris."

THE EL CHAPO REVIEW'S WEBSITE is unique, not only for its photograph of enormous stacks of U.S. dollars, but for the unusual wording of the payment terms they offered winners: "No contracts. El Chapo loathes contracts. He prefers paying cash money via PayPal. Payment will be made within 60 days of acceptance." This was a first. I've won a couple of essay contests and it's taken six months and a lot of reminders to receive my prize money.

I also appreciated the fact that there was no entry fee and that El Chapo "despises quid pro quo and reads blindly." It was nice to know some choke point in Chicago (the guy on the ground who pushes drugs for him) didn't have any better chance of winning the prize money than I did.

"All identifying information is to be removed," the website stated, which in this case seemed like a particularly good idea. Contest entrants were asked to be patient: "El Chapo anticipates an enormous amount of submissions and can only read so fast in prison." They claimed they would do everything they could to reply within one month, which I found impressive considering the plethora of submissions they were expecting. They also requested we not bother them with needless emails. "Please be patient," the website implored, "there is only one El Chapo."

At the bottom of the page was a final piece of edifying information that made me chuckle: "We're paying professional rates, so even if your essay was scribbled in the sand, it would be worth it. All rights revert to author so we might just scribble your piece in the sand, take some photos, then watch the waves swallow it."

IF WRITING FOR POSTERITY isn't important to a guy like El Chapo, I wondered, what is? Major-brand sneakers, I discovered, are apparently important to him. He reportedly owns more than seventy pairs of Nikes and Adidas. Maintaining and growing his markets worldwide for cocaine, heroin, methamphetamines, and marijuana, and bringing semiautomatic weapons and cash back to Mexico are important to him, as are eliminating his enemies and fingering high ranking government officials who accept bribes from him. Women are apparently important to Mr. Guzmán, who's had more wives than Donald Trump and more mistresses than Bill Clinton. But no matter what you think about the kind of business he's in, the number of victims he's claimed, or the extent of his womanizing, there's no denying that El Chapo's personal trajectory is a remarkable narrative.

BORN INTO EXTREME POVERTY in Badiraguato, a tiny town in the mountains of Sinaloa, and possessing only a first-grade education, Joaquín Guzmán Loera has appeared on *Forbes* magazine's annual list of billionaires four times since 2009. Like Steve Jobs, who didn't create them but radically improved our experience with personal computers and cell phones, Guzmán didn't create the drug-running business in Mexico. He merely figured out ways to improve and dominate it.

Opium poppies have been grown for export in El Chapo's home state of Sinaloa since World War II when they were used to make morphine for use on the European front. In the 1960s, Sinaloan farmers, including El Chapo's father, Emilio Guzmán Bustillos, expanded into growing and exporting marijuana for the rapidly growing U.S. market. At age fifteen, when his father squandered all of the money he'd made selling marijuana on alcohol and prostitutes, Joaquín began cultivating marijuana fields of his own to support the family. Through ruthless ambition, innate intelligence, and a series of lucky breaks El Chapo eventually became leader of the Sinaloa Cartel and a folk hero for many dispossessed people in Mexico. *Narcocorridos*, ballad-like songs about his life and deeds, abound on both sides of the border.

I WORRIED IT WAS UNCONSCIONABLE to submit to the *El Chapo Review* when cartels were known to murder journalists. Since 2000, more than a hundred journalists have been killed or disappeared in Mexico, many of them by narcos. Then I remembered the time in the 1960s when Joan Didion watched a five-year-old drop LSD during an interview in Haight-Ashbury and didn't call CPS. Instead she called the moment "pure gold."

In the end, my curiosity got the better of my conscience. I wanted to know if a literary review claiming to be operated by

El Chapo could possibly be real. And who—if anyone—would respond to my submission.

I EMAILED "DREAMING OF PARIS" to the *El Chapo Review* on October 14, 2016. I thought the essay, about my housekeeper Balbina's dream of seeing the Eiffel Tower before she dies, might resonate with Guzmán. Maybe it would remind him of his mother or his aunts or his grandmother. Or the many indigenous women in Mexico who lack the resources and education to realize their dreams. When I mentioned to Balbina that I wanted to send the essay to El Chapo, she replied: *"En su corazón, el Chapo es una buena persona. El ayuda muchos a los pobres en México."* Like many Mexicans, Balbina believes in the Robin Hood mythology surrounding Guzmán. I wasn't sure what to believe.

When a month passed and I still hadn't heard back, I went online to see if the review's website was still live and found something alarming: "If you haven't heard from us within a month, you're definitely in the running."

Oh my God! I thought. *What if the review is real and my submission is in the running?* Or worse: what if I actually won the contest? Having submitted merely to discover the truth about the *El Chapo Review*, I hadn't considered that possibility. Now my conscience was truly in a bind: I couldn't take money from a drug lord!

I imagined writing a scolding email to the *El Chapo Review,* telling them I would never accept their tainted money. Then I thought better of it. Maybe it would offend them, and this little query of mine might not end so well, given their dislike of journalists. I wouldn't feel good about taking drug money but decided that if by some chance the essay did win, I'd donate the proceeds to a drug rehabilitation facility.

Six more weeks passed and still no word. By this time, I was convinced it was a ruse. Then, on January 3, 2017, this popped up in my email inbox:

Dear Judith Gille,

Thank you for sending us 'Dreaming of Paris.' We appreciate the chance to read it. Unfortunately, the piece is not for us. Thanks again. Best of luck with this.

Sincerely,
Joaquín Archivaldo Guzmán Loera

I can't remember ever feeling so surprised or so relieved by a rejection letter.

Surprised because there it was: El Chapo's name on the email! And relieved that I wouldn't have to burden my conscience by accepting drug money.

Two weeks later, on January 15, I sent another essay to the *El Chapo Review*. This one was titled "Why Meditate?" I didn't send it because I thought it had the slightest chance of winning. I sent it because I thought it might prove useful to El Chapo, who, unless he manages to escape again, would likely be spending the rest of his life in prison.

Four days after I sent the second essay, Guzmán was extradited to the United States where he will stand trial in New York on seventeen counts, including murder, firearm violations, drug trafficking, money laundering, and extortion. He's also wanted on similar charges in five other states. According to prosecutors, if he's convicted, the charges in New York State alone would carry a minimum sentence of life in prison.

On January 26, I received the rejection for "Why Meditate?" I was expecting. This time the email was signed by a surrogate, not by Guzmán.

IN HIS INTERVIEW WITH SEAN PENN for the *Rolling Stone*, El Chapo presents himself as a simple, nonviolent guy just trying to keep his head down and make a buck. He also shrugged off any responsibility for the high level of drug addiction in the world today, saying: "Drug trafficking is already part of a culture that originated from the ancestors. The day I don't exist, it's not going to decrease in any way at all."

IN APRIL OF 2018, Duotrope warned authors off the *El Chapo Review*: "Do not submit here! This project is believed to be defunct!" it said. All in prominent red letters. But the *El Chapo Review*, apparently not ready to throw in the towel, tweeted this on May 8:

"We are still alive. Almost all our authors for Issue 1 have been paid in full. Looking forward to going live w/ a new site design. We pay professional rates. $100–$500. Highest paying online literary journal on Earth."

Almost all of their authors have been paid?

I MAY NEVER KNOW if the *El Chapo Review* is for real or not. But as I stare at an online photo of Guzmán in handcuffs and a puffy down coat the day he was escorted off a U.S. military plane in New York by two D.E.A. officers, I can't help but notice how much he looks like the rabbit my two dogs once cornered and I find myself hoping he saved a copy of "Why Meditate?" for future reference. I also kind of hope that the prison warden at Sing Sing, or wherever he ends up, allows him—if it is real—to maintain the *El Chapo Review*. I like imagining the world's most notorious drug-trafficker sitting cross-legged in his prison cell meditating, or with tortoiseshell reading glasses perched on his small nose, poring over dozens of carefully crafted essays.

I, however, will not be submitting to him again.

Disaster Gawking

THE SUNDAY BEFORE the 2016 election, I awoke in a panic. Like people who are prone to disaster-gawking, my mind gravitates toward worst-case scenarios. I can create train wrecks in my head over the most innocuous things and my overwrought brain was working overtime the Sunday before the election. Like millions of liberal Americans, I was obsessively checking Nate Silver's blog and was distressed to see Donald Trump's odds improving hour by hour. The week before, F.B.I. Director James Comey had sent a letter to Congress reopening Hillary Clinton's email controversy and her standing in the polls had been tanking ever since.

I imagined all kinds of Armageddon-style scenarios if Trump were to be elected: His tax cuts for the rich would lead to decreased funding for social safety nets, which would lead to increased homelessness and drug addiction. His promised ban on Muslims entering the country and mass deportations of Mexican and Central American migrant workers would lead to separation and severe hardships for families as well as labor shortages. There'd be stagnation, or even a lowering, of wages that would lead to riots, demonstrations, and increased violence, which would lead to increased surveillance and more military-style suppression. The N.R.A. would be emboldened and gun violence would worsen. Harassment of ethnic and religious minorities would increase multifold in the U.S. and across the globe because neo-Nazis everywhere would be bolstered by Trump's victory. The rich would continue to get richer and the poor poorer while the effects of climate change continued to wreak havoc on the planet. America would be looked down upon (or despised) by other Western democracies for electing a narcissistic demagogue as leader of the free world.

When I posted these worst fears of mine on Facebook, I immediately got pushback from many of my "friends."

"No way is that going to happen!"

"Trump will never be elected."

"Have faith in Hillary!"

A real friend messaged me to suggest I get off the Internet and do something more productive. *Not a bad idea,* I thought. Sitting at home, mired in anxiety about something I had no control over seemed absolutely senseless. At the exact moment I was trying to figure out what I could do that might actually be helpful, a reminder popped up in my calendar about the Latino Community Funds' Ballot Party—a call for volunteers to come support Latino voters in Seattle's South Park neighborhood. I shut down my computer, jumped in my car, and headed south to see if I could knock on doors, make phone calls, or help translate ballots for non-English speakers. Anything to help Latino voter turnout. A *New York Times* headline that very morning had given me hope: "Big Latino Turnout Breaks for Democrats." Having read, written about, and worked on immigrants' rights issues for the last ten years, I found it satisfying to think a surge in Latino voters might swing the election for the Dems and Hillary.

THE COMMUNITY OF SOUTH PARK is a twenty-minute drive from my apartment, but it feels light years away from Capitol Hill, the noisy, up-and-coming Seattle neighborhood where I live. The redevelopment and construction frenzy in my neighborhood has kept the area in flux, with rents climbing and longtime residents in a state of rage, for nearly ten years. By contrast, South Park feels like a place where time has stood still. Its single-story clapboard or brick houses and mature maple and elm trees remind me of the tiny suburb west of Chicago where my family lived when I was a kid. Like Westchester, the village of South Park was developed around World War II, in this case to house the rapidly growing Boeing workforce. Today, it's a no-man's-land, surrounded by a Boeing plant, Seattle's recycling center, and the massively polluted Duwamish River. This helps keep it off the radar of more affluent Seattleites and affordable for the forty-five hundred Hispanics who live there. The village's two centers of activity are its community center and library. When I arrived on that unseasonably sunny first Sunday in November, the community center was teeming with kids and adults taking dance classes, playing basketball inside and soccer outside, or attending the ballot party.

As is often the case with the volunteer work I do with migrants, I was the only Anglo in the room. Hispanic moms and dads, voting-age young people, grandmothers, and single men—laborers whose families were back in Mexico or Central America—sat at long tables while young children ran in and out of the room. No one greeted me or even looked my way, and it was soon clear that I had no useful role to play. I quietly asked an organizer if there was a plan to canvas the neighborhood that afternoon. He said no. The ballots didn't need interpreting. For the first time ever, the State of Washington had printed them in Spanish.

A representative from the Latino Community Fund was busy explaining the lengthy ballot to everyone in Spanish. Folks sitting around me looked confused when he explained that, in addition to voting on U.S. House, Senate, and Presidential candidates, there were a slew of judges, state legislature candidates, multiple local ballot initiatives, and recommendations to the legislature on the ballot. In Mexico, you vote for a president and maybe a senator, but ballot initiatives are unheard of and judges are appointed. Despite the long, confusing ballot, there was an abundance of energy in the room. Was it hope? Excitement? Nervousness? I wasn't sure. But when the moderator asked how many people were voting for the first time, over half raised their hands.

I WAS LISTENING IN, trying to decide whether to stay or go when everyone filed out of the room and lined up in the hallway. Lunch was being served as part of the ballot-party's offering, so I decided to stay and take part in the free Mexican buffet. When I returned to my seat a pretty young woman with waist-length black hair came over and sat down next to me. As we balanced plates filled with tacos, beans and rice on our laps, I initiated a conversation.

"¿Vas a votar?" I asked, wondering if she planned to vote.

She shook her head. "I wish I could, but I can't," she replied in Spanish. "I'm not a U.S. citizen." The young woman (whom I'll call Mónica in lieu of her real name), turned out to be friendly and forthright. She reminded me of Lupe, my closest Mexican friend and the mother of my three goddaughters. Mónica and Lupe were also the same age: thirty-one.

Mónica told me that she'd been born in Mexico, in the state of Tamaulipas. The state below Brownsville, Texas, where the Gulf Cartel, one of Mexico's largest and most violent drug cartels, has been in power since the early 1980s. In addition to drug trafficking, the Zetas—the military arm of the cartel—have a history of intimidating and torturing the local population. The Zetas are experts at extortion, kidnapping, and assassination.

"It became so dangerous in my town that my parents brought me to the U.S. when I was six years old," She said. She'd been raised in Texas by her father and grandmother after her mother—who'd married at age fourteen and had six children by the time she was in her early twenties—ran off with another man. As the oldest child in the family, Mónica had been left with the responsibility of raising her five younger siblings. Now that she had two sons of her own, one who was six and the other three years old, she told me she would never understand how her mother could have abandoned her children.

AFTER HER GRANDMOTHER DIED and her father moved to Alabama with his new wife, Mónica came to Seattle. She'd heard good things about the city: that they protected migrant workers and put limits on how much local law enforcement cooperated with *la migra* (Immigration and Custom Enforcement officials); that there were plenty of jobs, and a large migrant community where people helped each other. A few months after coming to Seattle she met her husband, who is also Mexican and undocumented. She told me that he worked three jobs to keep their small family afloat. Though currently at home with their two young sons, Monica dreamt of attending college when her youngest entered kindergarten.

"I want to be a social worker and help people," she said. "I hope to work at least part-time to help my husband pay the bills."

FOR THE NEXT HALF HOUR, we talked about many things: the challenges of becoming a U.S. citizen, whether or not she should apply for DACA (Deferred Action for Childhood Arrivals), and her husband's passion for salsa dancing which she didn't share.

"I have two left feet!" she said, laughing. Like their father, her sons loved dancing. Together we watched her two pint-sized boys—dressed like twins in crisp white shirts and gray trousers—getting their groove on at a kids' dance class in the room next door. But when Mónica tried to capture her sons' flashy moves on her iPhone, they both froze.

❀   ❀   ❀

AFTER LUNCH WAS FINISHED and those who were eligible to vote had filled out their ballots, we regrouped and marched together through South Park's leaf-covered streets toward the ballot box. As the cluster of thirty-some Latinos and one lone gringa gathered in front of the South Park Library on that brilliant, sun-filled afternoon it felt—at least for a moment—as if we'd transcended the hate, anger, and ugliness of the 2016 presidential campaign. The smiling faces of the people around me made me feel hopeful for the country and for our chances of winning the election. In that peaceful corner of Seattle, we celebrated America's great promise: an intact democracy, accessible to and inclusive of all people, no matter their race, ethnicity, history, or background. Each time someone dropped their ballot into the box, we cheered and clapped. We took photos, raised our fists, and proudly chanted, *"¡Sí, se puede!"* and *"¡Migrantes unidos jamás serán vencidos!"* Victory seemed so close.

❋   ❋   ❋

TWO WEEKS LATER, more than half of U.S. voters were still trying to cope with the shock and apprehension produced by the election results. I was trying to process my grief and anger about all we had lost or might soon lose. Instead of obsessing about polls, I began compulsively reading Facebook posts and news stories about the hatred and harassment being acted out by emboldened racists. In the ten days after the election, the Southern Poverty Law Center reported over 867 bias-related incidents: reports of black children being told to ride at the back of school buses; the words "Trump Nation" and "Whites Only" being painted on a church with a large immigrant congregation; a gay man being beaten nearly to death by a man who told him "the president says we can kill all you faggots now." I listened to harrowing stories on NPR: a woman wearing a hajib was threatened by a man who said that if she didn't remove her headscarf, he would burn her alive; a sixth-grader in Greenville, North Carolina, was taunted by kids who said he was going to be sent back to Mexico while he defended himself ("I'm an American, I was born here!"); a Trump voter in Nashville, who admitted that she actually liked her Mexican neighbors, but then added, "At least they're not Muslims."

Hearing, also on public radio, how Latino parents ended up in tears at a recent Seattle Public School District meeting intended to help undocumented parents navigate the changing political landscape. The school district's recommendations for these parents? Give their power of attorney to a legal citizen and provide emergency contact information to school officials, in case they get hauled off by I.C.E. while their children are in school. Evidently, even in a sanctuary city like Seattle, children could be separated from their parents in Trump-World.

IN AN ARTICLE IN THE NEW YORKER, columnist Francisco Goldman warned that the eight hundred thousand people who registered for DACA—Obama's program that exempted children from deportation if they were brought into the U.S. by undocumented parents—could now be sitting ducks. Their registration in a program that once brought them access to a college education, education loans, and hope for a better future was likely to become a deportation roster for Jeff Sessions, Trump's newly appointed Attorney General. People who've worked on immigrant rights for years were feeling particularly pessimistic. Heather Axford, an immigration attorney quoted in Goldman's article, said, "My job has always been difficult and stressful, but I'm afraid it's about to get tragic."

❈ ❈ ❈

SINCE ELECTION NIGHT, I have not been able to stop thinking about the many undocumented immigrants in the U.S. and what they might soon lose. All sense of safety and security; access to DACA, college educations, educational financing; the ability to pursue their dreams of obtaining a decent job and maybe a home; the freedom to speak out, to pursue citizenship, and to vote one day; any hope for a better life for themselves, their children, or their families back in Mexico, Central America, or wherever.

But what I fear most is that they (and the rest of the world) will lose faith in our American democracy. How do you explain to someone from places like Mexico or Central America, especially one who has never voted before, why a candidate who got nearly three million more votes than her opponent ended up losing the election? How do you describe the arcane details of our antiquated electoral college? What about the news of Russian interference in the election?

Is the U.S.—for all our sanctimonious talk about our Constitution and democratic principles—as corrupt as the countries these migrants left behind? And how are the criminal deeds and ambitions of our unprincipled president any different from those of the worst dictators: Chile's Augusto Pinochet or Argentina's Juan Perón? Anastasio Somoza of Nicaragua or Rafael Trujillo of the Dominican Republic? Or Porfirio Díaz, who ruled Mexico with an iron fist for forty years?

What is America, if not the nation of immigrants we have always claimed ourselves to be? Is "The New Colossus," Emma Lazarus's most famous sonnet, merely a quaint relic of an idealized past? Is the great American experiment in multiculturalism over?

If so, we are all losers. And America the biggest loser of all.

❋　❋　❋

TO THIS DAY, I continue to think about Mónica and her young family and wonder what happened to them. I worry that she could be sent back to Mexico, a country she hasn't seen since she was six years old and knows little about. Since I volunteer with an immigrant hotline, I know that, despite Seattle being a sanctuary city, I.C.E. sweeps are taking place every day and that *la migra* are hunting down and deporting hardworking people whose only crime is crossing the border without proper documentation.

I didn't get a chance to say a proper goodbye to Mónica that Sunday afternoon in South Park. I wanted to wish her well and tell her that I hoped she, too, would one day get a chance to proudly cast her ballot in an American election someday. But she'd hurried out the door that afternoon because her three-year-old son was throwing a tantrum. He wanted to keep on dancing and it was time to go home.

The Trouble with Walls—Part I

I will build a great wall—and nobody builds walls better than me, believe me—and I'll build them very inexpensively. I will build a great, great wall on our southern border, and I will make Mexico pay for that wall. Mark my words.

— Donald Trump, June 2015

FOR THE BETTER PART OF MY EIGHTEEN YEARS living in San Miguel, my Mexican friends and neighbors have, in general, shown more interest in American baseball than American politics. But Donald Trump, with his insistence on insulting them and building a border wall, has changed all that. It is not an overstatement to say that Trump, who they often refer to as *pinche Trump* (fucking Trump), has stirred up more animosity than any American president since James K. Polk, who invaded Mexico under false pretenses in April of 1846. President Polk turned a simple border skirmish along the Rio Grande into a war that would end with Mexico ceding nearly forty percent of its territory to the United States in the 1848 Treaty of Guadalupe Hidalgo. What follows here is an abbreviated history of the Mexican-American border and of a few border walls around the world. In case you're interested.

In the Beginning…

Undocumented immigrants flooded across a porous Texas border. In smaller towns immigrants outnumbered citizens by as much as four to one. Despite government decrees, assimilation was not happening, even among the people entering the country legally. Though the immigrants were well aware of government regulations requiring them to learn their adopted country's official language and abandon their old cultural traditions, they chose to disregard them. Two governments were locked in a standoff over issues of exports, tariffs, and unauthorized immigration. In response, one of them enacted more laws as a way of clamping down on the immigrants and the problems they were creating.

> — Gleaned from Lynn V. Foster's description of the Mexican territory of Texas in the 1820s in *A Brief History of Mexico*

(Note: The undocumented immigrants were Americans.)

A Lone Voice

Generally, the officers of the army were indifferent whether the annexation of Texas was consummated or not; but not so all of them. For myself, I was bitterly opposed to the measure, and to this day regard the war, which resulted, as one of the most unjust ever waged by a stronger against a weaker nation. It was an instance of a republic following the bad example of European monarchies, in not considering justice in their desire to acquire additional territory. Texas was originally a state belonging to the republic of Mexico . . . An empire in territory, it had but a very sparse population, until settled by Americans who had received authority from Mexico to colonize. These colonists paid very little attention to the supreme government and introduced slavery into the state almost from the start, though the constitution of Mexico did not, nor does it now, sanction that institution. . . The occupation, separation and annexation were, from the inception of the movement to its final consummation, a conspiracy to acquire territory out of which slave states might be formed for the American Union.

> — Ulysses Grant, From the *Personal Memoirs of Ulysses S. Grant*, 1885

Hadrian's Wall

According to his biographer, the Roman Emperor Hadrian was the "the first to build a Wall 80 miles long from sea to sea to separate the Romans from the barbarians." Hadrian's Wall was constructed around AD 122 and spanned northern England from the banks of the River Tyne on the North Sea to the Solway Firth on the Irish Sea. It had gates that functioned as custom posts and historians believe it to be one of the first frontier barriers constructed for the express purpose of border control.

The Tortilla Wall

In 1993, the year before the signing of NAFTA, President Bill Clinton ordered the construction of a border wall along a line in the sand between San Diego and Tijuana. It was the first officially mandated wall between Mexico and the United States. The fourteen-mile "Tortilla Wall" runs from the Otay Mesa Border Crossing and extends three hundred feet out into the Pacific Ocean. While there were other stretches of fence along the border before 1993, the Tortilla Wall is the longest official section to date. The Mexican side is covered with graffiti, crosses, photos and remembrances of undocumented migrant workers who died trying to reach the U.S.

❀   ❀   ❀

As ZAPATISTAS IN THE STATE OF CHIAPAS predicted, small-scale farming in Mexico was decimated as a result of NAFTA. In the years following the signing of the agreement in 1994, U.S. corn exports to Mexico increased by 300 percent. As a result, a new surge of immigrants in search of work headed northward into the United States, swamping border patrols and causing President Clinton to sign the Illegal Immigration Reform and Responsibility Act, increasing fines for illegal entry and approving funding for more patrols and fence construction. Migrants shifted from the traditional crossings to privately held land, causing landowners to fence their property.

Secure Fences

Mexican and Americans freely passed back and forth across the U.S.-Mexico border in the two centuries preceding September 11, 2001. After that, and for the first time in history, people crossing into the U.S. from Mexico were required to have a valid passport and, in the case of Mexican nationals, a visa which costs US$131 (16 percent of the average Mexican's monthly wage) and must be obtained through a U.S. embassy. In addition, on October 26, 2006, President George W. Bush signed the Secure Fence Act of 2006 into law, authorizing $1.2 billion to build seven hundred miles of additional fencing along the southern border. The law passed the Senate by a vote of 80–19.

The Great Wall of China

It is believed that construction on the first parts of The Great Wall of China began sometime around 770 BC, making it far older than Hadrian's Wall in northern England. The Great Wall of China is officially 13,170 miles long, but the portions at Badaling and Juyong Pass where tourists flock today were built during the Ming Dynasty (1368–1644). Measuring 5,500 miles long and spanning nine Chinese provinces, the Ming Wall is the longest contiguous wall in the world. Construction of China's wall continued on and off for twenty-two centuries.

The wall was initially built for defense purposes, to create a northern boundary line to help fend off marauding nomadic tribes, especially the Mongols. Later the Great Wall was used for border control and tariff collection; it allowed for the imposition of duties on goods transported along the Silk Road, regulation of trade, and control of immigration. The Great Wall of China was listed as a UNESCO World Heritage site in 1987. Despite popular misconception, the Great Wall cannot be seen from outer space by the naked eye.

✤ ✤ ✤

*If you are going to say that Mexico is not going to pay
for the wall, then I do not want to meet with you guys
anymore because I cannot live with that.*
— Donald Trump, in his first official phone call
with Mexican President Enrique Peña Nieto

The *Washington Post* reported that Peña Nieto considered
making an official visit to the White House in February or
March 2017, but Mexico and the U.S. both called the meeting
off after Trump refused to publicly affirm Mexico's position
that it would not pay for a wall at the U.S.-Mexico border.
The two presidents reportedly spoke by phone for nearly an
hour and neither would budge on the matter. For Mexico, the
wall is considered offensive; accepting it would be a blow to
national pride. For Trump, it is a campaign-trail crowd-pleaser
for die-hard supporters.

"The problem is that President Trump has painted himself, President Peña Nieto and the bilateral relationship into a
corner," Arturo Sarukhan, a former Mexican ambassador to the
U.S., told the *Post*. "From the get-go, the idea of Mexico paying
for the wall was never going to fly. His relationship with Mexico
isn't strategically driven. It's not even business; it's personal,
driven by motivations and triggers, and that's a huge problem.
It could end up with the U.S. asking itself, 'Who lost Mexico?'"

✤ ✤ ✤

BY 2011, THE DEPARTMENT OF HOMELAND SECURITY had completed 649 miles of barriers along the Arizona border, including
350 miles of pedestrian fencing, at an estimated $6.5 million
per mile, and 299 miles of vehicle barriers that cost approxi-
mately $1.7 million per mile for a total of almost $2.33 billion.
Trump projects his 2,000-mile fantasy wall will cost $12 billion.

Democrats say it's more like $70 billion. In September 2019, Trump stole $3.6 million more (for a total of $6.1 billion) from Defense Department projects to fund his wall, diverting money from much needed reconstruction projects including outdated bridges, dams, and levees in danger of collapse.

From the Guardian, October 4, 2016:
In 1989 there were 15 border walls in the world; today there are 70. Last year, countries as diverse as Austria, Bulgaria, Estonia, Hungary, Kenya, Saudi Arabia and Tunisia announced or began work on new border walls. There were a record 5,604 border deaths in 2015 according to the International Organization of Migration, and 65 million people displaced by conflict. These trends continued in 2016 with Bulgaria and Hungary expanding their fences, Pakistan building a fence on its Afghan border, and Britain constructing a wall in Calais, France to keep migrants away from the road leading to the Channel Tunnel.

❀ ❀ ❀

Just to add on, tremendous drugs pouring into the United States at levels that nobody has ever seen before. This has happened over the last three to four years in particular. The wall will stop much of the drugs from pouring into this country and poisoning our youth. We need the wall. It is imperative.
— Donald Trump's word-for-word remarks at a news conference with President Sauli Niinisto of Finland

From "5 Myths about The U.S.-Mexican Border"
by Wilson Center's Mexico Institute:
The top causes of [U.S.] opioid-related deaths in 2016 were, in order, synthetic opioids like fentanyl, prescription opioids and heroin. A large proportion of fentanyl is shipped by mail or express carrier directly from China. Some is trafficked through

Mexico, usually in vehicles through official crossings rather than in remote areas where a wall might complicate the smugglers' plans. Prescription opioids are produced and shipped through legal means. Finally, although heroin trafficking has evolved over the past decade to enter the United States mainly through Mexico, that drug, too, is primarily moved in vehicles through official crossings. Security improvements at ports of entry and cooperation with Mexican officials may contribute to a comprehensive anti-opioid strategy, but a border wall would not.

❀　❀　❀

The Berlin Wall

Unlike Hadrian's Wall, the Great Wall of China, and the Tortilla Wall, the Berlin Wall was built to keep people in, not out. After World War II, Germany was divided into four parts, each controlled by one of four Allied partners: Britain, France, the United States, and the Soviet Union. Berlin, one hundred miles inside the Soviet-controlled area, was divided into East and West. The West remained free and capitalist while the East fell under the control of the Soviets. Nikita Khrushchev once said that the existence of a conspicuously capitalist city deep inside communist East Germany "stuck like a bone in the craw of the Soviets."

By 1950, the majority of people living in East Germany aspired to independence and wanted the Soviets to leave. By 1953, over three million East German citizens, many of them skilled workers, had fled to the west. Fearing an increasing brain-drain, the East German government permanently closed the border between East and West Germany on August 13, 1961. It would not open again until November 9, 1989, when Guenter Schabowski, a Communist Party official, arrived at a news conference misinformed and mistakenly announced that a new law allowing East Germans to freely cross the border would take effect starting at midnight that night. The result was "the greatest street party in the history of the world" and the East German government would never regain control of the Berlin border again. This led to the reunification of Germany a year later.

❀ ❀ ❀

Now, we're going to build a real wall. We're going to build a wall that works, and it's going to have a huge impact on the inflow of drugs coming across. The wall is almost—that could be one of the main reasons you have to have it.
— Donald Trump, at a law enforcement rally

From the Brookings newsletter:
Drug smugglers have been using tunnels to get drugs into the United States ever since Mexico's most famous drug trafficker, Joaquín "El Chapo" Guzmán of the Sinaloa Cartel, pioneered the method in 1989. The sophistication of these tunnels has only grown over time. In April 2016, U.S. law enforcement officials discovered a drug tunnel that ran more than half a mile from Tijuana to San Diego and was equipped with ventilation vents, rails, and electricity. It is the longest such tunnel to be found so far, but one of 13 of great length and technological expertise discovered since 2006. Altogether, between 1990 and 2016, 224 tunnels have been unearthed at the U.S.–Mexico border.

❀ ❀ ❀

My friends think I'm crazy, but I love Donald Trump. He's the best thing that has happened to Mexico in a long time. Because of him, we are forced to let go of our attachment to the United States which has never been good for Mexico. We're finally forming trading alliances with other countries. Countries that respect us.
— Chiapan businesswoman in
San Cristóbal de las Casas, April 2018.

On May 8, 2019, the commerce journal *Business Insider* reported that there are now more Americans moving to Mexico than the other way around. According to a 2015 study from Mexico's National Institute of Statistics and Geography, more than half of the Americans living in Mexico are unauthorized immigrants or have errors with their paperwork.

From the San Diego Union-Tribune,
August 28, 2005:
Dave Smith, a professional acrobat and stuntman, successfully crossed the Mexican border in a unique way—shot from a cannon. Dave Smith, who bills himself as the "Human Cannonball," flew high into the sky and sailed 200 feet from the Mexican side to the American side of the border this afternoon as part of a performance art project, titled, "One Flew Over the Void," his publicist, Barbara Metz, said.

Smith was shot from Playas de Tijuana, just south of where the border fence disappears into the ocean and landed in Border Field State Park on the U.S. side of the border. He was unhurt. "He's a professional," Metz said.

❀   ❀   ❀

IN THE SPRING OF 2019, I volunteer to translate for an American medical team in Celaya, Mexico, tasked with ministering to people walking through Mexico with the "caravan." Among the patients we see are two teenage boys from Honduras with head contusions. They have walked nearly three thousand kilometers in flip-flops. When I ask how they got their head wounds they tell me a gang of Mexicans beat them up the night before.

❀   ❀   ❀

I MEET A MAN on the steps of the *biblioteca*, San Miguel's library, whose legs are missing from his mid-thigh on down. He has a tin cup set out to collect money. I sit down on the stairs next to him and we talk for a while. He tells me his legs were crushed when he fell under a freight train headed to the U.S. "I'm collecting money to buy prosthetic legs so I can go back to work *en el otro lado* someday," he tells me.

❀   ❀   ❀

THE GROUP BORDER ANGELS estimates that since 1994, about ten thousand people have died trying to cross into the U.S. from Mexico. According to the U.S. Customs and Border Protection, 7,216 people died crossing the U.S.-Mexico border between 1998 and 2017.

❀   ❀   ❀

EMPIRES RISE AND FALL. Once powerful nations or city-states have eventually tumbled into decline. Whole civilizations have disappeared over the course of history. Hadrian's Wall today is an impressively long pile of rubble that hikers use to guide them across the breadth of Northern England. Twenty-two percent of China's Great Wall has disappeared and what's left is now more tourist trap than transportation or customs corridor. The fall of the Berlin Wall and the political change that followed in much of Eastern Europe, including Germany and Poland, demonstrate that no matter how enduring governments or how solid walls may seem, they can always be brought down.

A #MeToo Near Miss

I.

I'VE PISSED OFF MY DAUGHTER. Alienated my son's girlfriend. Infuriated young women in my creative writing program. I even shocked my hairdresser, who is millennial, male, and Mexican, when I voiced my opinion about a twenty-two-year-old woman who claimed she was sexually abused by the actor Aziz Ansari. A recent encounter of my own had me thinking about the difference between sexual harassment, sexual abuse, and a hook-up gone awry. My encounter—which I've come to think of as a #MeToo near miss—happened on a trip to Mexico in the winter of 2018.

MY PLANE TO OAXACA was two hours late and by the time I arrived at Casa de las Bugambilias, the B&B inn where I was staying in the city's historic center, it was almost nine at night. After checking in, I enlisted the help of the desk clerk to help carry my oversized suitcase up to my room. As he and I (who, at five feet two, was a foot taller than he was) struggled to lug my fifty-pound bag up two flights of stairs, I admitted, rather sheepishly: *"Está llena de libros, soy una escritora."* As if the fact that I was an author with a bag full of books somehow excused the heft of our load.

Breathless from lugging the suitcase up two flights of stairs, I fiddled with the lock for a minute but the door wouldn't open. I called for the clerk to come back. He tried jiggling the key this way and that and finally the door opened onto a delightful room with brightly hued walls and a comfy-looking queen-size bed with a colorful Oaxacan headboard. *Heavenly!* I thought.

AFTER RUNNING A BRUSH through my limp, dirty hair and brushing my mossy-feeling teeth, I hustled downstairs. I was exhausted from the flights but even more hungry; I hadn't eaten since a light breakfast of yogurt and fruit twelve hours earlier. I was unhappy to discover that La Olla, the restaurant adjoining Las Bugambilias where I'd planned to grab a bowl of tortilla soup before collapsing in my room, was closed. I had to leave the hotel if I was going to find food that night. As I headed down the darkened corridor toward the front door, I heard footsteps behind me.

"Where are you going?" a male voice asked.

The light in the entryway was so dim that I could barely make out the man's face. But he sounded friendly enough. Assuming he was also a guest at Las Bugambilias, someone I was likely to see at the breakfast table the next morning, I decided not to snub him as I might have a stranger on the street.

"To get something to eat."

"May I join you?"

Before I could answer, a young man who looked eighteen or maybe nineteen years old appeared out of the shadows and inserted his body between mine and the stranger's.

"I'm Manoj," the man explained. "This is my son."

I introduced myself and shook Manoj's outstretched hand, but when I went to shake the boy's hand, he recoiled.

"I'm a little sick," he said.

"Sorry to hear that," I replied. "I hope it's not serious."

"No, just a little stomach trouble."

"Take some Pepto-Bismol," I said in a mother-knows-best voice. "I'm sure you'll feel better in the morning." With that, I headed out the door, leaving the kid and his dad behind.

It was January 6, El Día de los Reyes Magos in Mexico, and most restaurants were closed for the holiday. But across the street at the far end of the block, I found one that was open. I ordered *sopa de tortilla* and *garnachas* (small, thick corn tortillas) and fantasized about climbing into the comfy bed waiting for me in my room at Las Bugambilias. I'd just finished my soup and was working on my garnachas when Manoj walked in.

"There you are!" he called, as if we were longtime friends who'd gotten separated by accident. He hustled over to my table and pulled out the chair across from mine.

"May I?" he said, sitting down before I had a chance to respond.

Grudgingly, I nodded my consent. In the brightly lit restaurant, I could see he wasn't a menacing-looking character. In fact, he was fairly attractive with his smooth bald pate, large dark-brown eyes, and a sunny white smile which seemed stuck in a boyish grin. But it wasn't his looks that worried me, it was his overabundance of enthusiasm.

"Let's order mezcal," he said cheerfully. "It's my last night in Oaxaca!" Bypassing the waiter who spoke only Spanish, he got up and trotted over to the bar to get a recommendation from the bartender. He returned to the table, a shot of mezcal in each hand, looking very pleased with himself. Instead of joining him for shots, I ordered an odd cocktail made mostly of beet and tamarind juices with a little mezcal mixed in.

"So, I hear you're a writer," he said, leaning across the table.

I was taken aback. Freaked out, in fact. How the hell did he know this? I remembered telling the desk clerk that I was a writer, but I was certain I'd said it in Spanish and it was clear from Manoj's feeble attempts to engage the waiter that he didn't understand a lick of Spanish. I began to wonder if he'd grilled the desk clerk at the hotel for information or if this overeager stranger had Googled me.

"Yes, I am a writer," I said, feeling more reluctant by the second.

"That's why I'm so desperate to talk to you! I want to write a book, like you did. I need advice. Please, tell me everything you know."

Aha! All he wants from me is a little writerly advice, I remember thinking.

THIS BELIEF ALLOWED ME to maintain a level of equanimity as we politely summed up our bios for each other. He told me he'd been born in Madras to a Brahman family, but had left India at age seventeen to attend Yale and had never returned. From Yale, he went on to Harvard, where he got an MBA. He lived in Palo Alto, had founded and sold several start-ups, and was currently developing a product that would improve the intestinal biome of people with chronic intestinal disease. Being one of those people, I was all ears. I admit, until we'd gotten onto the subject of intestinal biomes, I'd been suspicious of his overly impressive CV. Among writers it's often said that the truth lies in the details. If it's the same for intestinal researchers, he was clearly telling the truth. He knew his biomes.

Unlike many of my other Indian American friends who immigrated to the U.S. around the same age, Manoj had absolutely no trace of India left in his voice. I asked him about this.

"I was young and wanted desperately to assimilate. I wore jeans, grew out my hair, and rid myself of my accent as fast as I could."

Forty years later, he was having regrets about turning his back on his culture. Despite his business success, he seemed to be at a loss for meaning in his life and thought writing a book would be a way to create the permanent legacy he hoped to leave behind. He claimed his business successes had made money but left him feeling empty. In his mind, returning to his birth culture and reengaging with Hinduism, and then writing about it, was a way to come to terms with the existential crisis he was experiencing. I reflected all of this back to him.

"Yes! That's it! That's what I want to write about!" he said, his enthusiasm ramping up again. "Tell me what I need to do."

HAVING EXPERIENCED MY OWN MIDLIFE CRISIS—one that had actually ended up launching a small writing career—I could empathize with Manoj. Plus, as someone who had led work-shops on writing and publishing for years, I was happy to share what I knew about the writer's life, even with a guy who seemed over-the-top intense.

"Read a lot and write every day," I said. "It takes ten thou-sand hours to master a new skill like writing, so you better not waste time." I recommended a number of craft books he might find helpful, names of authors who'd written similar books to what he hoped to write, and places where he might get help with his writing. I ended by sharing with him the same sage advice my writing mentor had told me early on.

"Don't quit your day job."

He laughed.

"I'm serious. Writing is a tough business. You won't make money at it."

"Money isn't an issue." This was confirmed when he later mentioned that his son was attending Brown University and his daughter would be at an equally expensive college next year. The fact that he didn't flinch at having to pay for tuition at two Ivy League colleges impressed me.

I'D FINISHED MY DINNER, paid my bill, and was about to return to the hotel when Manoj suggested we walk over to Alcalá, a walking street in central Oaxaca where he said a fiesta was going on. Being an amateur photographer, I'm always up for the photo ops Mexican festivals often provide. Still, I hesitated.

"Oh, come on," he said, "there's a big party going on over there. It'll be fun!"

"Okay, but only for a few minutes. I'm really tired."

We walked for a couple of blocks, but contrary to what he said, there were few people in the streets. The fiesta was over. Street vendors were packing up their stands for the night. Even the normally raucous bars in the area were quiet because of the holiday. As we walked along, Manoj tried slipping his arm around my shoulders a number of times but he removed it each time I was about to shake it off. Then, in the middle of Alcalá, he suddenly wrapped both of his arms around me and pulled me close.

"You've changed my life," he said, sounding serious.

"No, I haven't," I said, matching his seriousness while pushing him away.

"Why do you say that?"

"Because I can't change your life. Only *you* can change your life. I'm tired, I'm going back to the hotel now."

"Don't you want to have another drink? Look, the bar is still open up there," he said, pointing to the terrace at a restaurant named La Praga.

"No, I don't want a drink, I want to go to sleep."

I started walking in the direction of Las Bugambilias and he followed.

When we reached the hotel, the desk clerk had gone home for the night and the lights inside were turned down. If I'd been honeymooning, I would have thought it very romantic. As it was, I found myself fending off feelings of panic.

In the darkened dining room, as I was about to head up the stairs, Manoj grabbed me and wrapped his arms around me more tightly than before.

"When am I going to see you again?"

"Tomorrow morning at breakfast," I said firmly.

"But we're leaving early, before breakfast," he whisper-whined in my ear.

"Well, then good luck with that book, and don't forget to write every day!" I pulled myself loose and ran up the stairs, praying the room key would work. My hands trembled as I jiggled the key, first to the right and then to the left, until I found the magic spot and the door opened. Once inside, I doubled bolted the lock. But Manoj had not followed me up the stairs. I believe he went to his own room, like a good father should.

II.

A WEEK LATER I CAME ACROSS A STORY in the *New York Times* about a woman using the pseudonym "Grace" who claimed she'd been sexually abused by Aziz Ansari, another overzealous personality with a bright boyish grin. Grace's take on their date—as reported to a writer at the New York e-zine *Babe*—was that Ansari had taken advantage of her. Ansari, at least from the content of his text messages, was clueless about Grace's feelings. The gap between their perspectives of what happened was the size of the Grand Canyon.

You'd think my recent experience with Manoj might have made me sympathetic towards Grace, but it didn't. You'd think the fact that I've marched, rallied, and protested on behalf of women's issues for forty-plus years would have made me feel solidarity with Grace. It didn't. I've publicly fought for the E.R.A. (how many even remember what that is?), for abortion rights, for equal pay, for access to loans for women and minorities, for equal access for women in publishing and other creative endeavors. In my workplace—the first all-women-owned True Value Hardware store in the U.S.—I unflinchingly called out male employees for sexist behavior when I needed to and counselled them on what was and wasn't appropriate workplace behavior. I privately fought for respect in the hardware world and to be seen as more than a piece of ass by sexist men in that environment. Men have insulted, belittled, harassed, molested, slapped, and groped me. I've been thrown to the ground and, yes, forced to have sex against my will. Once.

AS THE GRACE VS. ANSARI DEBATE RAGED and pundits from nearly all major media outlets weighed in, I was reminded of two unhappy sexual encounters I'd had during a monthlong visit to the Greek Islands in the 1970s. The first was consensual and awful. The second was non-consensual and awful.

The first involved a guy named Josh. We'd first noticed each other at a café on the romantic, rugged island of Ios where I spent ten days in April 1976. Josh and I struck up a conversation which led to us spending the afternoon and evening together and, as so often happened in the pre-AIDS era, we ended up going back to his place and having what was, for me, distressingly rough sex. Afterwards, I felt sullied and used and, though it was well past midnight, I put on my clothes and walked the mile-long beach path back to my own rented room. I don't remember if Josh asked why I was leaving or if he even noticed. Oddly, what I do remember clearly about that night was sitting alone on the beach for a long time, staring at the strange neon-green glow of the surf as it washed ashore. I'd never seen bioluminescence.

Josh had given me his phone number in New York City and, as it turned out, I arrived at JFK with no cash and nowhere to go, so in desperation I phoned him, hoping I could stay at his place for a night or two until I figured things out. But Josh wasn't there and his father, after hearing how and where I'd met his son, was rude to the point of being hateful.

"And don't call back!" he'd said before slamming down the receiver.

I BLAMED MYSELF for the second sexual encounter—the non-consensual one—until one night in the summer of 1991 when I saw *Thelma & Louise* with my mother.

Deeply affected by the movie's final scene, I was still teary-eyed as we walked across the theater's parking lot. Judging by the set of her jaw, it was clear my mother did not feel the same way. When I asked what she thought of the movie, she said she felt no sympathy for Thelma (Geena Davis) who, in the movie, flirts with a guy in a bar who later tries to rape her in the bar's parking lot.

"That Thelma had it coming to her," my mother said.

"What do you mean she had it coming to her, how can you blame *her*?"

"She was acting like a harlot. Women who act like that are asking for it."

"It wasn't her fault! You have no idea what it's like to be in a situation like that," I said.

"And I suppose you do?" Her icy blue eyes cut right through me.

"As a matter of fact, I do."

I'd never discussed my sex life with my mother before; sex was a taboo subject in our conservative Midwestern household. But in the movie theater parking lot on that steamy Kansas night, there was no way of holding back the frustration and rage boiling up inside me. The emotional dam that had held my feelings in check for fifteen years broke wide open.

"I was raped in Greece," I blurted out. Then I explained how, due to a simple mistake any naïve traveler might have made, I'd ended up the victim of sexual assault.

I'D TAKEN A BUS FROM CHANIA, CRETE, early one morning with the plan of spending the day at Matala, a beautiful beach a couple of hours southeast of Crete's only major city. Matala was the place where Joni Mitchell lived in a cave for four months in 1966. The song "Carey," a favorite of mine from her album *Blue,* was about her time there. *Blue* was pivotal to my sense of self and the limited understanding of life I had at age twenty-two and I wanted to visit Matala as a tribute to her and to the times. But what started out as an innocent pilgrimage to a place popular with the free-love crowd in the 1960s turned into a very bad trip.

The rickety, noisy, smoke-filled bus I'd taken out of Chania bumped along Crete's narrow gravelly back roads, letting pas sengers off every ten or fifteen minutes. After two hours of stops and starts, I was the only soul left aboard. I knew no Greek other than *kali mera*, *kali spera*, and *efkaristo poly*, and had no way to confirm my destination. I repeated the word "Matala" to the driver several times. Finally, he pulled the bus over by an abandoned beach, cranked open the doors, and waved me off. When I looked at him questioningly, he pointed toward the beach, shouted something, and waved me off again.

I stepped down and wandered over to the small sandy beach where a lanky guy with a long brown ponytail and wire-rim glasses sat on a driftwood log, sketching. We struck up a conversation. He said he had no clue where Matala was but told me his name was Bill and that he made his living designing album covers for rock stars. Among the covers he'd designed was the one for Leo Kottke's *Greenhouse,* which I had in my record collection back home. Later that afternoon on the patio of the area's only house—a shack that doubled as a café by day—Bill and I ordered ouzo and shared a plate of *psari*, the tiny fried white fish popular in the Greek Isles. As we munched on the crispy little fish, I kept one eye on the road, watching for the bus back to Chania. It never came.

Night descended, the temperature dropped. All I had on were jean shorts and a thin cotton blouse. I was freezing. At his repeated urging, I crawled into Bill's sleeping bag. It didn't take long before he jumped in too and began groping me. I told him I wasn't interested, I only wanted to warm up. But he became more insistent, yanking at my shorts and shoving his erection against me, and I panicked. Bill was a big guy and far stronger than me. The beach was completely isolated. The shack-café dark. There was no one to call for help and nowhere to go. When he rolled on top of me and pinned me down, I gave in.

Afterwards, I climbed out of his sleeping bag and huddled in the sand all night, frozen with fear and cold. As soon as the sun came up the next morning, I hiked up a rocky precipice twenty minutes to the south and scrambled over the top. Below were dozens, maybe hundreds, of young people camping along a long black-sand beach. Salvation had been so close.

WATCHING THELMA & LOUISE triggered memories of that night and helped me understand what I had not been able to see before: What had happened to me was not my fault. I'd been forced to have sex against my will. Raped.

"For years I've blamed myself for what happened in Greece and I'm not going to do that anymore," I said to my mother in the movie theater parking lot. She turned and walked back to the car without a word and has refused to discuss sex or sexual abuse with me ever again. It was abundantly clear my words hadn't changed Mother's opinion that careless or "bad" girls get what they deserve, but they created a sea change in the way I thought about consent and abuse. Now, twenty-some years later, it's my thinking that seems antiquated, light-years behind the younger generation's.

III.

APPARENTLY, I WAS NOT THE ONLY MIDDLE-AGED WOMAN alienating young people over the Ansari debate. The blowback Caitlin Flanagan received for her article "The Humiliation of Aziz Ansari" in the *Atlantic* highlights the glaring generational divide between how baby boomers and younger women—particularly millennials—view male aggression and define victimization.

To me, the sex I had with Josh was awful, but it was consensual. Like Grace, I wasn't into rough sex. Ansari seemed as insensitive and oblivious to her needs as Josh had been to mine. I remember feeling cheapened by the encounter, as if I were being used solely for his pleasure, which most likely I was. But does that mean I was a victim? Was I abused? I could have gotten up and left, which is what I ultimately did. Still, would the young women at *Babe* define my experience with Josh as rape? As a #MeToo moment?

WOMEN MY AGE MORE OFTEN SEE MY EXPERIENCE and the Ansari affair the way I do: as a potentially good date—one we'd had big hopes for—gone awry.

"It was bad sex!" a friend said of the Ansari spectacle at a dinner party full of women who were red diaper babies, barrier breakers, and outspoken feminists.

"We had plenty of bad sex in the 1960s and 1970s... and, for that matter, in the 1980s and 1990s, too!" said another friend, throwing everyone around the table into fits of laughter.

One thing my friends and I did acknowledge that night: our expectations of how men would behave in bed were definitely not the same as they are for young women today.

"The bar was so much lower when we were young," Seattle's first female longshoreman, a woman who suffered continuous workplace harassment, reminded us that night.

No small number of women now old enough to join AARP have told me they experienced far worse things than what Grace did, and yet, like me, they refuse to think of themselves as victims. Especially if they considered the sex consensual.

This baby-boomer perspective of ours alienates younger women. When Caitlin Flanagan tried to explain in her *Atlantic* article why she didn't feel sorry for Grace, she got hurricane-like blowback from millennials. Like Flanagan, I believe that if Grace wasn't comfortable with what was happening, she should have told Ansari directly instead of insinuating it through the "non-verbal" cues she claims to have given him. Why didn't she just tell him no? I wondered. When I pondered this question over lunch one day with a twenty-nine-year-old friend in my MFA program at Bennington College—whose opinion and writing I greatly respect—she was appalled.

"It's never okay to blame the victim!" she snapped.

But in my mind Grace was not a victim. She was, at least at first, all-in, a willing participant. Just as I'd been a willing participant with Josh and, though less so, a willing participant that evening in Oaxaca with Manoj. I could have told him to get lost, but I didn't. I could have insisted on going back to the hotel after dinner, but I didn't. Instead I took a risk. Why? At least in part, because Manoj *flattered* me. Like Ansari, he was attractive and smart and rich and, in his particular case, knew more about intestinal biomes than anyone I'd ever met.

Still, I wonder. Am I being unsympathetic? Too quick to insist that Grace and I are not victims?

THINKING BACK TO THAT SUMMER NIGHT in the movie theater parking lot, when my mother told me Thelma got what she deserved, makes me wonder if I sound just like she did to the younger generation. Do I believe girls like Thelma and Grace and I deserve everything we get? *No, I don't.* So why am I being so hard on Grace? Or on myself, for that matter?

There is often a fine line between bad sex and abusive sex. (And just to clarify, I'm not talking about sexual assault or rape when I say bad sex—I have absolutely no problem calling them what they are: criminal acts of violence against women.) But where does the line get drawn between rowdy or lustful sex and abusive sex? Is it possible that what might come across as a frisky, fun sexual encounter to one woman would be considered abusive by another? Who gets to decide which is which? And why don't young women like Grace claim the agency young women today so often talk about when these situations arise? Why do they insist on seeing themselves as victims?

These questions bring up a bigger question: Why am I so opposed to women labeling themselves victims in cases involving ambiguous sexual encounters, which happen far more often than we like to think? Why am I so opposed to thinking of myself as a victim? What is it about victimhood that causes such an aversive reaction in me? I was clearly victimized by Bill that night in Greece.

Maybe it's because of the inherent power giveaway it implies.

I've spent my entire adult life trying to gain a small bit of power and respect, to be heard and seen in a world dominated by white males (remember I was in the *hardware* business). Acknowledging my victimization, I'm afraid, would feel like the moral equivalent of tucking my tail and running after years of fighting the good fight.

THE TRUTH IS ANYONE WHO ISN'T WHITE, male, and of the privileged class in this country is a victim. In the United States—where the personal interests and proclivities of well-educated, elite white men dominate—victimization is a given. As long as men still own or control or dominate every major corporation; 90 percent of financial resources in the U.S.; every female actor's, musician's, and athlete's career; the medical professions; all three branches of government; and most organized religions, women and minorities are going to be on the losing end of every battle. Whether it's a battle for reproductive rights, equal pay for equal work, or prison reform.

IV.

WHETHER MILLENNIALS, GEN-XERS, OR BABY BOOMERS, women have hard questions to ask of themselves, too. As the new feminist movement gains momentum and women assume more power, how we handle this new power is important. History shows that when classes of oppressed people gain the power they're not accustomed to possessing, one-time revolutionaries can become overzealous or obsessed with power, and lose track of the group's original goals and intentions.

It's also important for women to acknowledge the ways in which we participate in our own oppression. We continue to buy into standards of beauty, body size and shape that have no basis in reality. We support sexist, homophobic advertising campaigns. We buy products from companies that objectify women in their advertising and misuse them in the workplace. We listen to misogynistic music that celebrates violence against women. We dress and act the part of whore when that's what's demanded of us and are virgin-like when that's what is expected.

We defer to men instead of speaking our minds and continue to act in ways we think men prefer. Even when it goes against our better judgment and integrity.

Why, and for whose benefit, do we do these things? Why do we continue to participate in our own oppression?

I know I've been a willing participant in mine. Despite my age and experience, I still find myself acquiescing to powerful men. With fifty-plus years of relating to men and years of training in empowerment and human resources, it should have been easy for me to dismiss Manoj. To finish my dinner and go back to the hotel. But it wasn't. Maybe I wanted to please him. Maybe it was my infatuation with his credentials or the fact that he was rich. Maybe it was the pleasure I took in his fawning behavior. I don't know.

One thing I do know is this: my need for male approval and the lure of Manoj's success and authority played a role in that encounter. I lapsed into an acquiescent psychological state that night in Oaxaca that I, and every woman it happens to, should examine more closely. Because if our ego needs and desires are left unexamined, they can contribute to these highly charged sexual interactions and keep us from making decisions that allow us to engage in healthy, respectful sex and less able to disengage from abusive situations. Like Grace's, my ego wanted something from Manoj that night in Oaxaca. Had he been more aggressive, or I more submissive, our encounter might have turned into what my generation called a very bad trip and what women today call a #MeToo moment.

PART IV ✿ BENDICIONES

My friend Gracia and her husband Sebastian

We're all just walking each other home.
— Ram Dass

Chapulines

If you meet the Buddha on the road, kill him.
— *Lin Chi*

FROM AROUND THE age of three, the children of callejón Chepito play mostly unsupervised. Having lived on this Mexican alley for fifteen years, I know these kids well and enjoy watching them, though at times their games alarm me. Like Jack and his gang in *Lord of the Flies*, the boys on our alley sometimes make a blood sport of picking on younger, less capable children or other defenseless creatures. While younger kids might throw stones at or kick stray dogs, the older boys will toss firecrackers at cats and dogs or even unsuspecting foreigners who wander down the alley. I often ignore their miscreant activities because I don't believe in imposing my American values on my Mexican neighbors or their children. However, the day I caught the boys pulling the legs off a large grasshopper and snickering as the poor creature tried in vain to hop away, I couldn't help myself.

AT AGE FIFTY-FOUR, after a lifetime of hit-or-miss attempts at meditating and sorting through many of the world's religions, Buddhism surfaced as the spiritual tradition that makes the most sense to me. Theravada Buddhism, as practiced by most Westerners, is more a philosophy than a religion. It doesn't require you to worship deities, bow down to ancestors, or recite daily prayers. You don't have to worry about whether you're going to heaven or hell because, according to the dharma, you're already living in both places. The best part, as I see it, is that anyone can embrace the Buddha's teachings, even become enlightened. Because Buddhism is built on a foundation of practice, not blind faith.

Still, there are many aspects of Buddhist philosophy I find confusing. Such as how to interpret the Five Moral Precepts when you live in a modern Western society, and not a forest refuge in Thailand. Moral Precepts two, three, and four—abstaining from stealing, sexual misconduct, and lying—I'm pretty clear about. And I sometimes think that if the Buddha had ever tasted a fine Bordeaux, maybe he would have cut his adherents a little slack on number five: abstaining from intoxicants. But it's the first moral precept that consistently trips me up.

The Sanskrit word for the first precept is *ahimsa.* The word is often translated into English as nonviolence. In practice, it means doing no harm to others. Some people interpret it to mean doing no harm to mammals and people. Others, however, believe it means doing no harm to *any* sentient being.

Mahatma Gandhi was a consummate practitioner of ahimsa. In his autobiography, *The Story of My Experiments with Truth,* he explains: "The very fact of his living—eating, drinking and moving about—necessarily involves some himsa, destruction of life, be it ever so minute. A votary of ahimsa therefore remains true to his faith if the spring of all his actions is compassion, if he shuns to the best of his ability the destruction of the tiniest creature, tries to save it, and thus incessantly strives to be free from the deadly coil of himsa."

WHILE I ASPIRE TO PRACTICING AHIMSA according to how I think the Buddha or Gandhi might have, when my kitchen is overrun by sugar ants, or when yellow jackets threaten to carry our dinner away, I have been known to set out ant poison or hang wasp traps around the patio. Though it's a passive form of slaughter, I'm pretty certain these actions would, nonetheless, be considered part of what Gandhi called "the deadly coil of himsa."

I've had conversations with folks in my sangha—the Buddhist study group I'm part of—and with other Buddhists about the true meaning of ahimsa, which often result in me trying to rationalize the inconsistencies of my practice. My friend Barb once caught me at it.

"You Buddhists," she said, as I tried to explain why I kill some insects but not others, "you're all a bunch of hypocrites."

Though I knew she was joking, her words made me think harder about whether it was really necessary to kill ants and yellow jackets, or the scorpions that occasionally climb into bed with me at Casa Chepitos. After studying it further and giving it a lot of consideration, I resolved to take the bodhisat-tva's vow "to strive to work for the relief and liberation of all sentient beings," and, henceforth, refrain from killing *any* sentient being, including ants, yellow jackets, and other pesky creatures. However, when I took that vow of nonviolence I hadn't anticipated the Central Mexican locust plague of 2013.

NOT LONG AFTER I CHASTISED the boys on the callejón for tor-turing the grasshopper, I began to notice a preponderance of the jittery green insects in the alley. Not the normal Mexican *chapulines*, which are small and red and abundant in Oaxaca, where *campesinas* in the markets sell Ziploc bags full of them, but the large brownish-green ones that plagued my mother's garden and the farm behind our house in Kansas. Though I've lived part-time in Mexico for many years, I couldn't remem-ber ever seeing this kind of grasshopper on callejón Chepito. Like always, I ran across the alley to Gracia's store to ask her about it.

"Your problem is nothing!" she said. "In *el campo* outside San Miguel, the grasshoppers are destroying the *campesino's* bean crops."

The next day still more grasshoppers appeared in the alley. The third day a few had even taken up residence in the entryway of my house. But I didn't kill them. Like a patient aspiring Buddha, I grabbed a broom and swept them back out into the alley.

By the fourth day, the tops of two ficus trees in my inner courtyard were shivering under the weight of hundreds of the vile creatures.

I called my husband in Seattle, hoping he'd have some idea of how I could rid Casa Chepitos of the insects without killing them. He wasn't any help.

"Why don't you eat them," he suggested. "Like they do in Oaxaca. That way you can reconcile it with your Buddhist beliefs."

LATER THAT NIGHT I WENT ONLINE where I found some interesting—and a few decidedly disturbing—facts about grasshoppers. I learned that the beady-eyed, knob-kneed creatures crawling all over my ficus, dracaena, geraniums, and bougainvillea were *Schistocerca americana*, the American grasshopper. I also learned that there is no taxonomic difference between a grasshopper and a locust. According to a 2009 report in *Science*, grasshoppers are normally solitary and relatively harmless creatures. But a change in their brain chemistry turns them into the swarming pests we call locusts. Dr. Michael Anstey, the scientist who made the discovery, likened the grasshopper/locust phenomenon to the insect world's version of Dr. Jekyll and Mr. Hyde.

My online reading did not help. Instead, it made me rather hysterical. I lay awake half the night remembering the chapter from *On the Banks of Plum Creek* (by Laura Ingalls Wilder of *Little House on the Prairie* fame) where swarms of locusts descend on Pa's wheat crop. I could still picture Ma and Pa Ingalls running around like lunatics setting grass fires in their fields to chase away the locusts. All to no avail. Their farm gets wiped out. I finally fell asleep, still wondering what my beautiful Mexican house would look like when the plants were completely denuded like Pa's fields and Ma's vegetable garden.

THE NEXT MORNING, I headed downstairs to the kitchen and found myself eye-to-eye with a grasshopper perched on the tap of my water dispenser. A giant olive-colored female. (In my Internet search, I'd learned that a female's abdomen is jagged whereas a male's is smooth.) She stared me down with her bulging black eyes and dared me to touch her. While working up the courage to grab her and toss her outside, I suddenly noticed a persistent *tap, tap, tapping* on the windows, as if hail or giant raindrops were striking them. *That's strange,* I thought. *It's sunny outside, there's not a cloud in the sky.* I pulled aside the curtain on the front door and saw dozens of grasshoppers heaving their bodies against the glass: an all-male squadron, I was sure, since autumn is mating season for the resolute buggers. I spent the morning sneaking in and out of side doors and keeping the front door and unscreened windows tightly closed. I was determined to keep my new housemate in and her horny boyfriends out. No way did I want her laying her eggs anywhere near my house or garden.

When Balbina and her son José Luis arrived to clean the house and tend the garden, I tried to loop them in on my little scheme.

"*Por favor*, would you mind keeping the doors closed today?" I said, sheepishly pointing to the grasshopper still glued to my watercooler's tap. "*Quiero proteger a este chapulín.*"

Balbina's eyebrows shot up when I told her I was intent on protecting a grasshopper, but neither she nor José Luis questioned my peculiar request.

TO GET OUT OF THEIR WAY and get some work done myself, I grabbed my laptop and headed upstairs to the terrace. With its lovely view and leafy, peaceful ambiance, the highest point of my Mexican home is a sanctuary.

Not that day.

The minute I opened the door, grasshoppers—now transformed into swarming Mr. Hydes—whizzed by like miniature projectiles. They landed on my shoulders, on my head, on my neck. They grabbed at my clothing and my hair with their tiny terrible claws. They scattered across the floor, clung to walls, perched on the loveseat and chaise lounge. They were making themselves at home in my pots and chewing the life out of the dracaena, the ficus, and my beautiful hot-pink bougainvillea.

The sheer number of skittery insects caused my aspiring bodhisattva-self to snap. Grabbing a flip-flop from my foot, I began swatting at them with the rage of someone who should be medicated. I tripped over a table, crashed into pots, knocked a candle sconce off the wall. With each fresh kill, pale green slime oozed out and stuck to the sole of my flip-flop, but the gruesome goo didn't deter me. I kept swinging as locusts zipped around, frantically trying to escape my determined *thwacks*.

Hearing my shrieks and the crash of furniture, Balbina ran up the stairs. José Luis was right behind her. Seeing me barefooted and red-faced, gripping a slimy sandal, I think frightened José Luis. He stared at the mess I'd made and glanced nervously at his mother. But Balbina didn't flinch. She simply shrugged and started sweeping up the carcasses scattered across the terracotta tiles. After the initial shock of seeing his employer looking so deranged wore off, José Luis set to work, watering the half-eaten plants.

IN THE ALLEY LATER THAT AFTERNOON, I told Gracia and the two Señoras Rosas about my battle with the grasshoppers up on the terrace. The Señora Rosa who lives to the north of Casa Chepitos looked rather gleeful as I described my troubles.

"I don't have a single one in *my* garden," she said in a tone that sounded a lot like gloating. "They must to prefer yours."

I told Gracia that I was seriously considering hiring the boys on the alley to be my hit men.

"I could pay them a peso per bug to round them up," I said, although it later occurred to me that rounding up that much small change in Mexico might be as challenging as killing the bugs myself.

The next morning, around ten o'clock, my doorbell rang.

"We're here to take care of the grasshoppers," Gracia announced. She had a commercial coffee can with a red plastic lid tucked under her arm as she pushed her way past me into the house. In lieu of the neighborhood boys, she had every one of her own children and grandchildren in tow. Marcos, Marthín, Cholo, Lupe, Juan, Gisela, and Juana Judith followed her through the door and up the spiral staircase to the terrace.

Gracia and the guys set right to work killing the multitude of locusts still clinging to plants and covering the walls, but Lupe and six-year-old Gisela were squeamish. They squealed in unison each time they smashed a locust or when one jumped close to them. My namesake, Juana Judith, who was now two years old and full of herself, delighted in the slaughter. She stomped on grasshoppers with cheerful abandon and fell into fits of giggles watching Lupe jump and shriek and shake grasshoppers out of her long black hair. Clearly Juana Judith enjoyed the aggressive nature of our "game."

Lupe looked at me, worried I'd be horrified by my goddaughter's unladylike behavior. In this case, my response was decidedly more feminist than Buddhist.

"A little aggression in a girl is good," I told Lupe. "It's still a man's world out there."

By the time the second killing spree was over, we'd cut the locust population to a fraction of what it had been. Gracia opened the giant coffee can full of dead and dying bodies, but no one had the stomach to count them. Instead of doling out pesos, Lupe and I trotted down to the market where I bought a dozen Milanesa sandwiches at our favorite *torta* stand. We carried them back up the hill and distributed them to our legion of locust dispatchers, who were tired and hungry from the morning's mission.

MONTHS LATER, BACK IN SEATTLE, I admitted to my friend Barb that I'd broken my vow of non-harming and told her the grass-hopper story. She laughed.

"Most Buddhists are pragmatists at heart," she said. Then she told me a story about an ancient monk she'd met while visiting a Buddhist temple in Myanmar. Smoking was strictly forbidden for temple residents, but the monk, realizing Barb was not a practicing Buddhist, reached under his saffron robes and pulled out a pack of Marlboros. "Would you like a smoke?"

"IF YOU MEET THE BUDDHA on the road, kill him" is a famous Zen koan attributed to the ninth century Buddhist monk Lin Chi. Like other koans, it was not meant to be taken literally. Koans are riddles or puzzles that can lead to greater insight if meditated upon rather than reasoned out. There are probably as many interpretations of Lin Chi's koan as there are Buddhists in the world, but my take on it is that if we identify too much with the Buddha or become preoccupied with the correctness of Buddhist thought, we've missed the point of the enlightened one's teachings. Awareness is born of letting go, not of clinging to notions about our ego-selves or the attainment of perfection.

In his book *Mindfulness*, dharma teacher Joseph Goldstein writes: "If practicing the precepts doesn't make us uncomfort-able, it's probably a sign that we should investigate them more deeply." When I now find myself obsessing about some aspect of the teachings, or worried too much about my own Buddha nature, I figure it's time to return to my meditation cushion.

THE NEXT TIME I ENCOUNTERED THE BOYS killing grasshoppers in the alley, I changed my strategy. Instead of chastising them or chasing them off, I suggested we feed the carcasses to our neighbor Maria's duck. Pelousa loves fresh bugs and sits by the front gate for hours, her bright orange bill sticking out under-neath, waiting to be served fresh "meat." It might not be totally in keeping with the spirit of ahimsa, but it feels better to me.

The Night Billy Collins
Stole Alejandra's Poem

THE EVENING BEGAN with Billy Collins's keynote address to a standing room only crowd at the San Miguel Writers' Conference. It was really more a poetry reading than a typical keynote, but it didn't matter. San Miguel's expat community is an easy crowd. We're polite and enthusiastic and appreciate when big-name authors come to San Miguel and wax on about the charming colonial hill town we've adopted as our own. It vindicates our decision to have uprooted our lives in the U.S. or Canada, leaving old friends, family, and all that is familiar to settle in an overcrowded, mid-sized Mexican town with no Costco or Home Depot, but with a big heart and an even bigger expatriate community.

True to form that night, Collins read with great aplomb and gently mocked his audience as is his style. I guess when you're seventy-six, have a hot new girlfriend who looks thirty years your junior, and have received every poetry honor under the sun, including being appointed Poet Laureate of the United States, you can tease your fans with impunity. The lampooned audience lapped it up, laughing along in a good-natured way and applauding loud and long when the reading ended.

AFTERWARDS, WHILE COLLINS signed books and amused his readers with acerbic remarks, I met up with my friend and houseguest Alejandra. Like Billy, Alejandra is a poet. A Latinx American poet who was born in Mexico but now resides in Eastern Washington. We met in the summer of 2016 at a writers'

conference in Port Townsend, Washington, and bonded immediately. For her, the trip to San Miguel was significantly more
important than merely attending another writers' conference:
it was her first time back in Mexico after twenty-five-years.

OUR PLAN FOR THE EVENING was to attend the keynote
after-party—a private event held at an ex-Northwest art deal-
er's elegant San Miguel home to celebrate Collins and other
conference luminaries.

Due to the size of my annual tithe to San Miguel's Literary
Sala I receive invitations to a few private events. However,
my tithe is not large enough to include a guest, so we had to
sneak Alejandra into the party that night. Problem is, it's hard
to "sneak" someone as lively and outspoken as Alejandra in
anywhere, though she did once sneak into the United States.

Twenty-five years ago, she crossed the border with
her ex-husband who—a number of years and three babies
later—abandoned his family. Both he and Alejandra were
undocumented when they arrived and lived under the Fed's
radar for years. But after her husband left, Alejandra managed
to obtain a green card and worked as many as three jobs at once
to support her three children. When the kids were older, she
went back to school, earned a master's degree in Multicultural
English Literature, and now teaches at the Heritage College in
Yakima. She's fought breast cancer, ICE, the U.S. Department
of Customs and Immigration, and has beaten all of them. She's
smart, pretty, forthright, and, as of last summer, a U.S. citizen,
who sounds a lot like the actress Sofia Vergara when she talks.

WHEN COLLINS FINALLY FINISHED signing books and arrived at
the party, Alejandra charged over to him.

"Billy Collins, you stole my poem!"

Billy and his girlfriend happened to be staying five doors
down from us on callejón Chepito in a sumptuous stone and
stucco house designed and owned by an architect from Boulder

and his wife. That evening, Billy had read a new poem he'd written about San Miguel. The poem offset the idyllic beauty of the house and neighborhood with the reality of life on our alley and in Mexico: barking dogs, feral cats, raucous roosters, blaring music, clamorous church bells, and nightly explosions of firecrackers. The audience roared in recognition.

"I have no idea what you're talking about," he said, sizing up Alejandra over the top of his black-rimmed Warby Parkers.

"I'm staying on callejón Chepito, just like you," she said. "And I wrote a poem about the dogs and the roosters and the loud music, too!"

Alejandra—who was staying in the front bedroom at Casa Chepitos and being awakened at four a.m. by the same noisy cat fights and time-challenged roosters as Collins—had written her own poem satirizing the illusory paradise of our lovely Mexican callejón.

"Well, I wrote it first," Billy said with a smug grin.

Remembering "Drinking Alone," a popular poem he'd read that night, with its subtitle "After Li Po," Alejandra had a quick comeback: "Then I will call my poem 'After Billy Collins'!"

"You can do that," he said.

Alejandra and I laughed about their little dustup all the way home. We loved the sullen expression on Billy's face; the shocked expressions on the faces of the guests standing nearby; how Collins acted as if he couldn't understand her English; her quick comeback at the end. Every little aspect of her tiff with Billy Collins struck us as hysterical. On our way up back home, we laughed like a couple of slaphappy drunks. Alejandra abstains from alcohol, but I don't and I was a tipsy from the glasses of white wine I drank at the party as we staggered down callejón Chepito in a state of riotous laughter.

Death Comes to the Callejón

The night Billy Collins stole Alejandra's poem was also the night my neighbor Bernardo died. Nearly three years later, the disparity between how the evening began and how it ended stands out in my memory as a lesson in how fleeting the moment—and even life itself—can be.

ALEJANDRA AND I are halfway down the alley when I spot a large group of glum-looking people assembled outside my front door. Seeing them sobers me right up. In fact, it makes me downright uneasy. Something I don't often feel in my Mexican neighborhood after fifteen years. But more than half of my neighbors—Marcos, Martín, Gracia, Cholo, Balbino, Marcelo, Oscar, Rolando, Julián, Julito, Soledad, Pancho, Susana, Delia, and a number of others I don't know—are sitting or standing quietly outside my door, as if in a trance or under some spell and this alarms me. It takes a minute or two for me to realize it isn't the size of the crowd or the fact that they're camped out in front of my door that makes me uneasy, it's their *silence*.

Mexico is not a quiet place and those of us who live along callejón Chepito are not quiet people. When my neighbors and I assemble, no matter how small our number, the decibel level is high, as the two-meter space between the houses echoes with lively conversation, raucous laughter, or tunes blasting from iPhones or radios. Unlike the deathlike suburban stillness I grew up with in Kansas, silence in Mexico is an anomaly. It means "something is not right."

Gracia—our alley's unofficial spokeswoman and my closest ally—steps forward to explain.

"Judith, tengo noticias muy tristes," she says, looking as if she might cry. *"Bernardo murió."*

Like everyone else, I'm suddenly speechless. The news that my neighbor Bernardo—a thirty-some-year-old father of four—is dead seems inconceivable. I've known Bernardo since he was a kid. My son Will played baseball with him when they were teenagers, and Bernardo continued to play ball and lead an active, vigorous life. He was popular with everyone in the callejón and always greeted me warmly whenever I returned to Casa Chepitos, wanting to know what "Guillermo" was up to, and how my family was doing. I'd had a long conversation with him only two days before. While I remembered him looking as if the air had been sucked out of him, he hardly seemed on the brink of death. He told me he was headed up to the General Hospital to spell his wife, who'd been there for twenty-four hours straight with their critically ill infant. Still, I'm unable to wrap my head around the idea that Bernardo is *gone.*

My disbelief is laid to rest minutes later when two funeral home employees arrive with his body in a box. The highly polished wooden coffin is strapped onto a foldable metal gurney which they roll down the alleyway and through the gate leading to his home, directly across from mine. Watching the deftness and speed with which the men work, I realize how often they are called on to perform. And, as the coffin is carried into the house, how much closer Mexicans are to their dead than we Americans are to ours.

OVER THE NEXT TWO DAYS people file in and out of the house where Bernardo lies in repose behind a plexiglass window in the satin-lined coffin. The man behind the glass doesn't look like Bernardo as much as a simulacrum of him, a mustachioed figure made of wax that belongs in one of Madame Tussauds' museums. Alejandra—who is horrified by the specter of a dead body on view in someone's home—stays behind at Casa Chepitos. Her reaction strikes me as incongruous; she was, after all, born and raised in Mexico where it's customary to keep the bodies of deceased family members on display in the home for two or three days. But I'm also aware that Alejandra's entire adulthood has been spent in the United States where we make a great effort to put as much distance as possible between ourselves and death.

I bring flowers to Bernardo's widow but can't provide much comfort to his grieving family. Being so choked up, I can't find the words in Spanish to express my regrets. Then again, the proper words on such occasions frequently escape me, no matter what language I'm speaking.

LATER, I ASK GRACIA what Bernardo died of and she shakes her head. She doesn't know. No one seems to know. Even Bernardo's family can't explain the exact cause of his death. If a thirty-eight-year-old man died in a U.S. hospital, you can bet family members would demand to know the cause of death and it would be explained in detail by the doctor himself. And if the family didn't get the answers they wanted or trust the doctor did everything in his or her power to save their loved one, they might sue the doctor or the hospital. It would never occur to my Mexican neighbors to sue the doctor. They're more likely to tell you "it was God's will."

Among expats, rumors circulate about how and why Bernardo died. Some say he'd used a chemical on plants in the gardens of homes where he worked that destroyed his lungs. Others say he was denied treatment at the General Hospital that could have saved him because he was poor and couldn't pay. One woman tells me she heard the hospital had a machine that could have saved his life but it was not used because it cost fifty thousand pesos. Many Americans living in San Miguel believe Mexican doctors and hospitals favor patients who have money and give them preferential treatment while denying or ignoring the needs of the poor.

I have limited experience with doctors in San Miguel, or with its General Hospital.

I don't know if doctors adhere to the Hippocratic oath with any consistency here, or if they adhere to it at all. What I do know is that if there is anything equivalent to the Hill-Burton Act—the federal law passed by the U.S. Congress in 1946 requiring hospitals to treat everyone who walks through their doors—my Mexican neighbors don't know about it and that most hospitals here insist on being paid up front. When Marco's ex-girlfriend Verónica was due to deliver her baby at the General Hospital, they demanded payment in full before they would admit her. We started a small fundraising campaign on the callejón when our neighborhood garbage collector, Balbino, needed surgery he had to pay the full bill up front.

ON FRIDAY THAT WEEK, every Mexican on callejón Chepito and a handful of Americans who employed Bernardo show up for his funeral procession, which begins on the Cuesta de San José and ends at the Panteón de Nuestra Señora de Guadalupe behind the Real de Minas Hotel. A mariachi band plays melancholy music as we trail the hearse through the streets of *el centro*, down Zacateros and the Ancha San Antonio, to the cemetery. A small group of men dressed in drag tag along behind the crowd. Bernardo was a member of a group of neighborhood guys who dress up as women and dance in the annual *LOCOS* parade celebrating San Antonio de Padua in late June. At the cemetery they will perform one last crazy dance to honor their friend.

As our small crowd of mourners file past the Instituto Allende on the Ancha, I am haunted by the memory of an incident that happened some forty years ago, when I was a student at the Instituto.

❋ ❋ ❋

I'D ENROLLED IN A PHOTOGRAPHY CLASS and, one day, my teacher—a hulking, sandy-haired guy named Jay—took our class up to Atascadero to photograph the desert. We spent most of the morning wandering listlessly around, looking for interest-ing shots when suddenly, on a cactus-covered hill directly above us, an old-fashioned horse-drawn cart bearing a coffin appeared. The horse and cart bumped slowly along a rugged road as a small cortege of black-clad mourners trailed behind.

"An amazing shot!" Jay exclaimed. And it was. The wagon and mourners were silhouetted against a crisp blue sky offset by the stark desert landscape. Jay commanded us to hustle up there and snap some shots before the entourage moved out of range. I balked. I was uncomfortable with the idea and staged a weak protest.

"You'll never be a real photographer if you're too scared to get up close for a shot," Jay responded. His words struck me as a double-dare might strike a ten-year-old.

FOUR OR FIVE OF US SCRAMBLED over boulders, around agave and sagebrush and nopal cactus to catch up with the cortege. Having only a 50mm lens I had to move in closer than the other students who had fancier zoom lenses. While attempting to adjust the camera's f-stop for the shot, I noticed a man in the cortege pick-ing up a large rock. He quickly picked up another and hurled them both in our direction, narrowly missing my head.

Today, I deeply regret chasing after that cortege with my camera in hand—not because a rock narrowly missed my head, but because I now understand how profoundly disrespectful it was to the mourners that day. A moral position I was either too meek, too naïve, or too egotistical to defend at age twenty.

❀   ❀   ❀

THERE IS A DHARMA LESSON about the inevitability of death in a story I've often heard in meditation circles. A ninety-five-year-old man went to the doctor for what he thought was some minor problem. After running some tests, the doctor discovered the man had an aggressive form of cancer. When he gave the man the bad news, the old man looked toward the heavens and asked: "Why me?" At this point, everyone in the meditation hall usually breaks into laughter. But don't we all asked that question, when a death sentence of a diagnosis is delivered to us or to a loved one?

I'm tempted to ask, "Why Bernardo?" just like I do each time a child or young person dies, or a dear friend receives a terrible diagnosis.

"THE CRADLE ROCKS ABOVE AN ABYSS," writes Vladimir Nabokov in his memoir, *Speak, Memory*, "and common sense tells us that our existence is but a crack of light between two eternities of darkness. Although the two are identical twins, man, as a rule, views the prenatal abyss with more calm than the one he is headed for." Nabokov goes on to write about his surprise when, as a child, he discovered photos from before he was born, and realized there was a time when he hadn't existed. Part of his juvenile realization was the awareness that someday he would, again, cease to exist.

From the day we are born—as Nabokov so eloquently points out—we are on a trajectory toward death. The 7.7 billion of us who inhabit this planet have little choice about when or how we will die. But one thing is certain: the poorer we are, the fewer choices we have. We might be in our thirties, like poor Bernardo or my friend Chip, who died at thirty-eight from HIV-related illness. Or in our sixties like the majority of people—sixty-nine is the current life expectancy worldwide. Or over one hundred, as my mother will likely be when she passes.

So, what do we do with the knowledge that our existence is but a brief crack of light?

For me, the important question isn't when or how I'm going to die. It's this: What do I want to do in the days or months or years I have left to live? How do I want to spend this precious time? Do I want to spend my remaining time fretting about everything that could and will go wrong with me? Or can I live more fully and generously than that? And, when my time does come, will I be able to find a way to face the inevitable with grace and equanimity?

El Día de los Muertos

I T'S NOVEMBER 1—the Day of the Dead—a time when people throughout Mexico create elaborate altars in homes, businesses, and on graves at cemeteries to honor the dead. Markets are full of bright orange cempasúchitl, magenta celosia, and sweet-smelling tuberose. Tables loaded with decorated sugar skulls, skeletons, even lambs made of icing sugar appear in pop-up markets around San Miguel. We paint our faces up like skeletons, don our finest suits or dresses, and parade through the streets. We visit *ofrendas,* elaborate altars created by schools and community groups around the San Juan del Dios church and the Panteón de la Guadalupe cemetery, where graves adorned with flowers, candles, and tequila entice the spirits of deceased family members to return.

IN THE ALLEY, just outside my front door, Bernardo's family has created an altar honoring him. In the center is a photo of Bernardo, with his large round deep-brown eyes and bushy black brow, smiling broadly and wearing a red polo shirt with CANADA printed across the front in giant white letters. The altar is embellished with the traditional items: fuzzy cockscomb and huge orange marigolds, votive candles, yellow and purple and pink *papeles picados,* sugar skulls, several bottles of beer, a glass of water (or maybe tequila?), peanuts in the shell, and a sweet roll. There's also a sugar *borrego,* a lamb to guide Bernardo up to heaven. My contribution to the altar is talking Sebastian into donating a baseball on the promise that I'll replace it with one Ichiro signed (which I, to date, have yet to locate). Bernardo loved baseball.

Two weeks earlier, my friends Laurie and Larry and I had walked over to the cemetery. Bernardo worked for them for eight years and they wanted to pay their respects since they weren't able to be in San Miguel for his funeral. Laurie carried a large bouquet of purple and yellow chrysanthemums that she wanted to place on his grave, but the three of us ended up wandering haplessly around for twenty minutes or more, unable to find the grave. For good reason.

MEXICAN PANTEONES ARE NOT LIKE OTHER North American cemeteries, at least not like those in the U.S. or Canada. Instead of being spacious and green—with neatly mown lawns and carefully tended graves, each marked with etched marble headstones lined up in exacting rows—a Mexican cemetery, like Mexican culture, is colorful and chaotic. San Miguel's Panteón de la Guadalupe is a hodgepodge of wrought iron fences surrounding tightly packed graves adorned with real and fake flowers or floral streamers; or red, white, and green plastic flags snapping in the breeze; stone statues of angels or Jesus or the Virgin of Guadalupe; and irregular rows of monolithic marble or concrete tombs. Crammed in between all of this are simple mounds of dirt with humble hand-painted crosses or ceramic blonde-haired, blue-eyed angel figurines—the latter often adorning the graves of children or babies.

Having attended the funeral seven months earlier, I had a vague memory of where Bernardo's grave was. We combed the area where I thought it should be but we still couldn't locate it. I remembered a rusty black wrought iron fence and a simple hand-painted cross in lieu of an expensive stone marker. What I'd forgotten was that he was buried on top of two family members. His grave marker was buried beneath those of his wife's father and uncle.

＊　＊　＊

I'VE JUST CUT INTO MY VEGGIE OMELET at the Café Santa Ana when the doors to the *biblioteca's* lecture hall are thrown open and dozens of people file out dressed in black T-shirts bearing the colorful logo from Pixar's new movie *Coco*. A truly cosmo-politan crowd.

In addition to Spanish, I hear French, Italian, Portuguese, and English being spoken. The international set mills around the small café for a long time and, from what I can glean, they are awaiting instructions for their next move. Curious to know who they are and what they're up to, I strike up a conversation with a woman from Paris.

"*Nous faisons de la publicité et promotion international pour les films,*" she says. (We do publicity and marketing for films internationally.)

They are here in San Miguel for a screening of *Coco*, she says, and to experience the "real" Día de los Muertos. Their next stop is a makeup-artist's studio where they will have their faces painted up like *calacas* before participating in the Day of the Dead parade through town that night.

LATER THAT EVENING, my friend Thomas and I walk down to the *jardín* to watch the Muertos parade. The place is jam-packed with people, having their faces painted at curbside *puestos* or eating *elote*, tacos, and ice cream. Finally, the parade arrives. Eighty percent of the people cruising past us are foreigners, and right in the middle of them, I spot the *Coco* promotion crew with their black T-shirts and brightly painted skeleton faces. The Frenchwoman I met at the biblioteca, along with the others, looks as if she is having the time of her life. "*Qui savait que la morte pouvait apporter telle joie?*" I imagine her telling friends back in France. (Who knew death could bring such joy?)

＊　＊　＊

THE FOLLOWING NIGHT, I take Lupe, Juan, and their three daughters (my godchildren) to see *Coco* at the Cinemex theater. *Coco* is the first Pixar movie to have a Mexican protagonist and I am determined that my girls—who have never been to a movie theater—are going to see it. Evidently, I'm not alone. The first night we try, the place is so full of people that tickets sell out before we get to the kiosk. We purchase tickets for the following night and show up early so we can get our gallon-size buckets of buttery popcorn and 24-ounce Coca-Colas before they sell out too.

IN HER NEW YORKER ARTICLE, "Coco, A Story about Borders and Love, is a Definitive Movie for This Moment," Jia Tolentino had this to say about Pixar's new hit film: "*Coco* is a movie about borders more than anything—the beauty in their porousness, and the absolute pain produced when a border locks you away from your family."

With an amazing soundtrack and visually stunning animation, it's an easy movie to love. But beneath its festiveness and feel-good moments, the movie's themes are a heartrending commentary on Trump's anti-immigrant campaign. Given the recent separation of children from their parents and the incarceration of families who are seeking asylum in the U.S. from violence in Central America, the movie seems as relevant today as Orwell's allegorical novel *Animal Farm* was in Europe in 1945, after fascism nearly destroyed democracy in the world. But for most of my Mexican friends, the movie's big takeaway is far simpler: families belong together and sometimes members have to make sacrifices in order to keep them together.

WHATEVER THE TAKEAWAY, by the end of the movie the sleeve of my sweatshirt is drenched in tears. Outside the theater, on our way to the bus stop, I can't stop thinking about the Mexican family members trapped on the far side of the border as Trump wages his personal war on migrant workers. When I completely break down, Lupe puts her arms around me.

"The idea that people working in the U.S. can no longer see their families in Mexico breaks my heart," I tell my friend, who illegally crossed the border herself ten years ago and knows how tough being separated from your family can be. "What if you and Juan hadn't been able to get back?" By now my three young goddaughters are crying, too. We all wrap ourselves up in a giant group hug and sob.

The Trouble with Walls—Part II

I N EARLY 2017, as liberal America waged its war against Trump and his inane border wall, I became engaged in my own personal battle with walls. I'm staunchly opposed to Trump's wall, as are all of my Mexican neighbors and 99 percent of my American friends, a few of whom insist I shouldn't be discussing my little wall issue in the same breath as the great border wall debate. As my daughter might say, mine is such a "first world" problem. Still, as Trump's border wall with Mexico became the hot-button issue in American politics, walls simultaneously became a major theme in my personal life. It began when the vacant lot below Casa Chepitos, my home in San Miguel de Allende, was sold.

Our Fantasy, Crushed

FOR YEARS MY HUSBAND PAUL AND I HAD FANTASIZED about buying the property below ours, not only to protect our Mexican home's lovely view (for which I named a memoir), but to plant a garden and small orchard of citrus and avocado trees. In 2015, I reached out to the owners through my friend Gracia and her husband, Sebastian, who had known the family since childhood. However, upon seeing my gringa face, the sellers jacked up the asking price to more than twice what adjacent properties of the same size had sold for the very same year. Not having that kind of disposable income, and with a daughter to put through college, it wasn't in the cards.

A couple of years later, when Gracia informed me that the lot had been sold, I went on a mission to meet the new owner and find out what he had in mind for the property. Since Gracia personally knows everyone who lives within a five-mile radius of callejón Chepito (and to bolster my courage), I asked her to come along. Rumor had it the property's new owner was renting a house off callejón Landín, the alley directly below ours.

WE STOPPED BY THE HOUSE OF A WOMAN who lived in the middle of Landín, and was, of course, nother longtime acquaintance of Gracia's. She told us an older gentleman "who speaks Spanish fluently but is not Mexican" had bought the property below ours and pointed to the house where he was currently renting. Gracia and I walked over and knocked on the door expecting an older non-Mexican man, but instead a young Mexican man answered the door. After we explained who we were and what we wanted, he asked us to wait outside. Twenty minutes later, a fastidious little man with thinning gray hair and a thick accent arrived. I introduced myself and pointed uphill to show him where I lived and then explained why I was there.

"I'm Berny," he said. "It's spelled with a *y*." He confirmed that, indeed, he planned to build. I then politely asked if Berny with a *y* and his architect could take our home and its view into consideration when siting and designing his new house.

"I know exactly what the rules are and how high I can build," he said firmly. He opened the door to his rental wider and invited me in to take a look. A massive brick wall completely blocked the view from a bank of six-foot-tall windows.

"This is what people do here. Everyone wants to take advantage of the views." Then he added: "If you didn't want someone building in front of you, you should have bought the property yourself."

DISHEARTENED, I SHUFFLED BACK TO CASA CHEPITOS, hoping against hope that I'd made an impression on Berny and that, despite his response, he'd be inspired to build a low-slung, ranch-style house like the Mexican woman to the south of his new property had.

Killing Trees Does Matter

IN OCTOBER OF 2017, three young men arrived and began chopping down the trees below our house. Trees that had been home to red-winged blackbirds, vermilion flycatchers, woodpeckers, goldfinches, and kingbirds. Twenty-foot-tall Peruvian pepper, mesquite, and jacaranda trees that had created a feathery green canopy in front of our house for sixteen years. I watched in tears as they hacked away at the trees' branches and ravaged their trunks with anemic chainsaws. When I said to the one guy within hearing range that it was sad to see trees I'd lived with and loved for sixteen years being cut down, his response was *"Ni modo."* But it did matter. To me.

SHORTLY AFTER ALL OF THE TREES below my Mexican home were chopped down and hauled away, a crew of *albañiles* showed up to excavate a foundation for a dividing wall between the properties. I freaked out. The hole they were digging abutted my retaining wall and was three feet from my house, which would be illegal most places in the U.S. In Mexico, however, building codes are often nonexistent or not enforced even when they do exist. I had been well aware that the new wall would likely block the view and light from my living room, but, as my neighbor's perimeter wall inched higher and higher, I worried it was going to block the view from the master bedroom, too.

I consulted Gracia's husband, Sebastian, who informed me that the maximum height limit for walls in San Miguel is eight and a half meters. He also said the city would enforce them, especially if there were complaints. I then talked to a couple gringos who'd battled Mexican developers over height restrictions: one had won his case, the other lost. I frantically dropped a fifty-foot tape measure out of my bedroom window to see if I even had a case. From the ground, eight and a half meters (27.88 feet) came to just below the master bedroom's window seat. The one that overlooks the steeples and domes of San Miguel's many churches, the steely waters of the Presa de Allende, the gray-green hills of Guanajuato. I breathed a little easier.

War Zone

ONCE STARTED, CONSTRUCTION ON THE WALL and house dragged on for months. I awoke each morning to a pounding so intense that I felt as if I lived in a war zone. All morning long, it sounded like bombs were being detonated below my bedroom window. Work started at eight a.m. or earlier and sometimes continued until eight p.m. Dust from the mixing of concrete covered every horizontal surface inside the house and most of the plants in my garden. The workers trampled my plants, destroyed a ficus tree, filled my small patio with rubble. They smoked dope and played the weirdest mix of music—from old Eagles pop tunes to reggaetón to Mexican boleros—at a feverish volume. After six weeks of this, my nerves were completely jangled. The construction ruckus became so unbearable, I began going down to Starbucks on the jardín every day to write. When I arrived home one day to discover that my gardener had butchered the last remaining ficus on my patio because "the new neighbor told him to," I exploded. I later apologized profusely but asked José Luís to please confirm any further pruning projects with *me*.

THAT NIGHT I LAY AWAKE—my anger and frustration spinning out of control—imaging all sorts of bad things happening to the man responsible for so negatively impacting my peaceful Mexican life. I imagined him dropping dead of a heart attack. Becoming so disabled by a stroke that he could no longer walk uphill. Being roughed up by the gang of tough boys who live on Landín and deciding the alley was far too dangerous. A little too gleefully, I fantasized about buying a voodoo doll, naming it Berny, and sticking pins in it.

Enough already! my better nature shouted, interrupting the downward spiral my anxiety-driven ego was on that night. *You sound just like Donald Trump, the other asshole you love to hate.*

Stuck in Mexico

IN EARLY MARCH, DESPERATE FOR A BREAK from the dust and the noise and the acrid smell of marijuana mixed with fresh concrete, I booked a flight back to Seattle for ten days. But at the airport in Mexico City, I was blocked from boarding the airplane by an Alaska Airlines clerk who insisted that I report immediately to an immigration official at the INM office downstairs.

In an ironic twist, it turned out I was not allowed to leave Mexico. I'd applied to become a permanent resident of Mexico and, after three months of waiting, still had not received my ID card.

"I could give you a tourist visa, but if I do, your application will be invalidated," the INM officer said in Spanish.

THE WOMAN I'D HIRED TO HELP ME with the application had failed to mention one small detail: I was not allowed to leave or reenter the country without that card. But I wasn't angry; I wasn't even upset. I figured my problems were nothing compared to the problems Mexicans and other immigrants were experiencing. Plus, with all the stupid anti-immigrant vitriole in the United States, I decided I'd rather be stuck on the Mexican side of Trump's wall. The "fun side" as a sign in one San Miguel café says.

My New BFF

OVER THE NEXT FEW WEEKS, while I awaited the card that would permit me to return to the U.S., Berny began stopping by Casa Chepitos for regular visits. If the doorbell rang before nine a.m., I could pretty much bet it would be him. The man I was prepared to hate (or, at least, dislike intensely) turned out to be pleasant and helpful. When I showed him the mess on my side of the new wall, he ordered his workers to clean it up. When I complained that his roof's design was likely to block the view from the master bedroom, he changed it. When I asked if the workers could play their music at a slightly lower volume, it was quiet the next day. Berny was Colombian American, multilingual, charming, and funny. He'd led an interesting life as a trauma surgeon, was a great storyteller, and reminded me of my husband's grandfather. By the end of April, we were fast friends and I felt ashamed of the terrible things I'd imagined happening to him. And my new friend also, inadvertently, taught my ego to take a joke.

IT HAPPENED ONE DAY, when on my way down to the jardín with friends, I ran into him on the Cuesta de San José. I'd given him a copy of my memoir *The View from Casa Chepitos* a few days earlier and he told me he was enjoying it so much that he'd recommended it to his friend Clay who had also recently bought property on callejón Landín.

"But his copy is the new edition," Berny said.

"There is no new edition," I replied.

"Oh yes, there is. Clay sent me a photo of it."

He searched his phone and finally pulled up the image he was looking for: an image of my book, but in lieu of the image of San Miguel's Parroquia on the cover, there was a photo of a roughly mortared brick wall with the title and subtitle of my book superimposed on it. Even the award sticker was there. Below *The View from Casa Chepitos*, this was added in pink letters: *2018 Edition.*

I was outraged. Someone had stolen my memoir! I was ready to track the pirate down and threaten them with a lawsuit when it dawned on me: it was a joke. Doh! When I Googled him, it turned out Berny's friend was a world-class photographer who, evidently, also had a great command of Photoshop. That Berny and I had both been duped by the parody was a testament to the guy's abilities.

A Blank Slate

I OBSESSED ABOUT WHAT TO DO with the blank slate that now stretched across the front of my property and was eight-and-a-half-feet tall. I visited the homes of friends and friends of friends to see various artistic treatments they'd done on their walls; I consulted Anado McLauchlin, San Miguel's renowned mosaic artist; I discussed the problem of my blank wall with several friends who suggested everything from planting a green wall to installing a giant horizontal wall fountain. Berny had many suggestions for what I should do on my side of his wall but the idea of a mural was his favorite. Paul also liked the idea of a mural; he thought we should hire an artist to paint a picture of the view we used to have. I wandered around San Miguel's Guadalupe and San Antonio neighborhoods photographing the colorful murals. In barrios outside of the *centro histórico*—where there's a prohibition on signs, paint colors, and artistic expression—there's been an explosion of fabulous public wall art.

In the end I bought two large boxes of colored chalk and invited the kids from the callejón who came to my sixty-fifth birthday party to decorate the wall. Aged three to thirteen, they embraced the art project with zeal. By the end of the evening my slate was no longer blank—it was covered with birthday greetings in Spanish and English, fanciful flowers, colorful birds, smiley faces, stick figures, odd geometric shapes, and horse-like creatures I suspected were unicorns. When Berny arrived an hour later with a box of the finest chocolates from Joffrey's in hand, he gave a gleeful thumbs-up to the young artists and their handiwork.

Good Fences, Good Neighbors?

I DON'T BELIEVE THAT GOOD FENCES MAKE GOOD NEIGHBORS. This tired old maxim was first introduced into the national zeitgeist by the recalcitrant neighbor in Robert Frost's 1914 poem "Mending Walls," and remains a rallying cry for people mainly interested in protecting their own self-interests.

But I also don't believe walls necessarily make bad neighbors. What make bad neighbors are people with character traits such as arrogance, insensitivity, and selfishness. Traits on full display in the United States right now. My experience with my new neighbor and his wall helped me see that I can choose to be like that, or I can choose to be an ambassador for the character traits I'd prefer to see Americans, especially our President, embrace more wholeheartedly: empathy, tolerance, humility, generosity, and fairness.

❀ ACKNOWLEDGMENTS ❀

First, I want to thank my mother, for instilling in me a sense of wonder and curiosity about the world. At 100 years old, she's the best example I know of how to live a long and productive life: Stay interested in the world around you, work crossword puzzles every day and don't stress out about dying!

It takes a village to write a book and lots of villagers contrib-uted their expertise to this one.

I owe much gratitude to my editor and friend, Frances Woods, for her insightful edits and ongoing support. And to Griselda Robles for her help editing the Spanish and enthusiasm for my stories.

I also want to thank Clifford Thompson, Ben Anastas and Jill McCorkle, my mentors at Bennington College, for their help with these essays and stories. I am, as always, indebted to The Shipping Group in Seattle for their suggestions and encouragement over the years. And especially to the group's generous leader, Waverly Fitzgerald, who passed away this past December. She will be missed by many in Seattle's writing community. Also, a big thank you to Patty Garcia for working yet more magic in the design of this book.

Last, I want to thank both of my families: Will, Hannah and Paul Atlas and my Mexican family, the Cordova-Rodriguez clan. Their love, friendship and support mean the world to me.

❀ ABOUT THE AUTHOR ❀

Judith Gille's work has appeared in *The New York Times, The Los Angeles Times, The Dallas Morning News, the South Florida Sun-Sentinel* and in numerous magazines, online literary journals and in anthologies. Her memoir, *The View from Casa Chepitos: A Journey Beyond the Border,* won Writer's Digest's Grand Prize in 2013 and a Nautilus Award. She holds an MFA in Creative Writing from Bennington College and teaches at the San Miguel Writers' Conference.

www.ingramcontent.com/pod-product-compliance
Lightning Source LLC
Chambersburg PA
CBHW022007080426
42733CB00007B/515